TWENTY-FOURTH EDITION
REVISED

●

How to Make

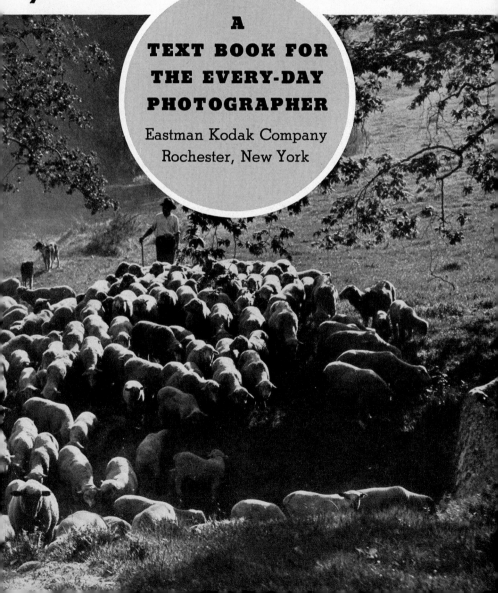

Good Pictures

A TEXT BOOK FOR THE EVERY-DAY PHOTOGRAPHER

Eastman Kodak Company
Rochester, New York

INDEX

LEFT: *"Back" lighting adds charm to this story-telling scenic, as well as to the one on the preceding page.*

The

"THE CALLER"
Story-telling pictures are interesting to everyone.

Book

ITS title quite fully explains its mission. While "How to Make Good Pictures" treats only of "still" photography, the movie camera enthusiast will also find much of interest in it. This twenty-fourth revised edition is quite in step with photographic progress and contains much that did not appear in previous editions.

Prominence has been given to the Kodak system of picture making as time has demonstrated its supremacy for the producing of fine results in the easiest way.

A HELPFUL SERVICE

Even though all of the essential directions for obtaining good pictures are given in this book, further information on _any_ subject in photography may be obtained through correspondence with the Service Department, Eastman Kodak Company, Rochester, N. Y. If you would like helpful, constructive criticism of your work, send along negatives and prints. There will be no charge— no obligation.

IF YOU WOULD KNOW MORE OF THE
"WHYS AND WHEREFORES"

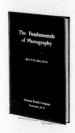

A knowledge of the theory of photography is by no means essential for making fine pictures — even masterpieces, but if you have a curiosity about the scientific side, procure "The Fundamentals of Photography" by C. E. K. Mees, D. Sc. In simple language this book provides an elementary account of the theoretical foundations of photography as well as an interesting bit of its history.

EASTMAN KODAK COMPANY, Rochester, N. Y.

PICTURE MAKING TODAY

THERE is a new fascination to amateur photography. Pictures that but a few years ago would not have been attempted are now easy snapshots. Even striking and unusual pictures are now made by the novice. As you turn from chapter to chapter in this book you will readily realize that the scope of photography has broadened tremendously and that the usefulness of the camera has increased a hundredfold with the result that picture making today is a more intriguing hobby than ever.

No need now to wait for sunny days or to miss a single picture opportunity on your day off or over the week-end because of dull skies. Modern cameras will work for you indoors or out, day or night, summer or winter; regardless of the hour, they can be made to produce exceptionally good pictures. Study all those reproduced in this book — they show a wide range of picture possibilities, in daytime — from early morning to sunset—and at night outdoors and indoors.

LEFT: *Earliest extant picture of a human face made by photography. Taken in 1840 in glaring sunlight, face coated with white powder. Exposure ten* MINUTES. *Today snapshots,* SPLIT SECOND *exposures, are made indoors, at night, of vivacious children, even with simple box type cameras loaded with "SS" Film, and using No. 2 Photoflood bulbs.*

Back in the sixties the traveling photographer had to carry along his tent dark-room to coat and develop his big, heavy "wet" plates en route.

With but very little of the "knowing how," anyone can secure results similar to the pictures shown throughout this book.

THE REASONS WHY

By gradual improvement, refinement, and simplification in camera design and the recent introduction of remarkable new films Kodak photography today is sure and simple. All this has come about not in a day or week, but through years of constant endeavor on the part of scientists and practical workers. Cameras are more compact, lenses are faster. Accessories for special effects have been introduced. Developing, printing and enlarging, always interesting, have been simplified and fine results made surer for the amateur. Practically all of the splendid examples of artistic photography we see in salons and on

the walls of camera clubs today originated with a small, compact type of camera.

This shows how the snap-shot on page 8 was made with a camera having f.6.3 lens, loaded with Kodak "SS" Film. The bulbs in the home lamps were replaced with No. 1 Photo-flood bulbs.

9

HOW A CAMERA "WORKS"

WHAT HAPPENS WHEN A PICTURE IS TAKEN

Bʀɪᴇғʟʏ, ʜᴇʀᴇ ᴀʀᴇ ᴛʜᴇ ғᴀᴄᴛs. While a knowledge of the theory of photography is, today, in no way essential for taking good pictures—even from the start—some readers may like a concise, elemental explanation.

First then, let us take a look, with "x-ray eyes," at a simple camera (see diagram at right). You see that it is by no means intricate; the basic principles of construction are quite easy to understand.

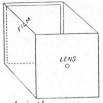

A simple camera.

The crudest camera would be just such a box, made light tight, a lens at one end and a means for supporting a light-sensitive film at the other.

THE BELLOWS

The bellows used on folding cameras takes the place of the light tight box and permits the camera to fold up, thus helping toward compactness. It also provides a means for setting the lens at different distances on certain "focusing" cameras.

The bellows permits the camera to be collapsible.

THE LENS

The purpose of the lens is to form a sharp image of the objects you want to photograph and to project the picture image onto

10

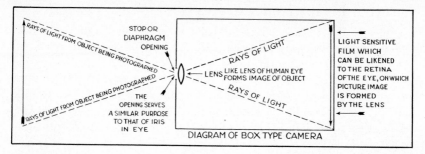

RAYS OF LIGHT FROM OBJECT BEING PHOTOGRAPHED

STOP OR DIAPHRAGM OPENING

RAYS OF LIGHT

LENS LIKE LENS OF HUMAN EYE FORMS IMAGE OF OBJECT

RAYS OF LIGHT

LIGHT SENSITIVE FILM WHICH CAN BE LIKENED TO THE RETINA OF THE EYE, ON WHICH PICTURE IMAGE IS FORMED BY THE LENS

THE OPENING SERVES A SIMILAR PURPOSE TO THAT OF IRIS IN EYE

RAYS OF LIGHT FROM OBJECT BEING PHOTOGRAPHED

DIAGRAM OF BOX TYPE CAMERA

the sensitive film at the back of the camera.

The simplest means we could use for a camera lens would be a very small hole, made with a pin or needle, in the front of the box where the lens would ordinarily be. Because it takes a long time for sufficient light to pass through such a small hole to record a picture on the sensitive film, a lens is used.

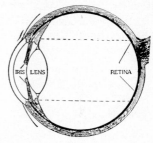

IRIS LENS RETINA

How the eye resembles a camera. Dotted lines indicate shape of camera.

THE SHUTTER

Showing the adjustable iris diaphragm in a Kodak shutter.

The shutter is a mechanism for allowing light to pass through the lens for definite periods of time, seconds and split seconds, though there is also an adjustment on most shutters to keep them open as long as desired for a "time" exposure. There are different kinds of shutters, but they all perform the same service.

DIAPHRAGM OR "STOP" OPENING

The diaphragm or stop opening in the shutter controls the *volume* of light admitted through the lens to the light-sensitive film at the back of the camera.

The range of sharpness in a picture is also dependent upon the size of the opening—the smaller the hole, the greater the "depth" or range of sharpness of objects at different distances from the camera. (See page 39 about an interesting and instructive experiment.)

11

EFFECT OF LIGHT ON THE FILM

The film which is placed at the back of the camera to make the negative is coated on one side with a light-sensitive substance known as the "emulsion," and when an image is flashed on this sensitive coating by the light that is admitted through the lens, a chemical change takes place. No change, however, is noticeable to the eye should we examine the exposed film in the darkroom by the aid of a photographic safelight. Nevertheless, an invisible image has been formed and this invisible picture, or "latent" image as it is called, can not be brought out except by a further chemical change; this change is made by placing the film in a solution known as the "developer."

After the image has been made visible the film must then be placed in another solution in order to make the negative image permanent. This solution is called the "fixing" bath. The term "fixing" is used because the bath *"fixes"* the picture, so it will not fade out.

THE NEGATIVE AND THE PRINT

After you have fixed, washed, and dried the developed film, which is now called a "negative," because the dark objects appear light and the light objects dark, you get the final picture by another process called "printing." A sensitized photographic paper is placed in contact with the negative and exposed to a light for a certain period of time. The paper then goes through solutions which act like those which were used to obtain the negative, and a print or picture results.

LEFT: *A negative image. Tones in a negative are the reverse of those in the objects we take pictures of; whites are black, blacks are white.*

RIGHT: *A positive image: When we make a print from the negative, things become as they originally appeared and we have a true picture.*

THE CAMERA FOR YOU

You probably have a camera, but if it is not up to date you may want a modern model; one with greater capabilities or one of another size to supplement your present outfit. Here then are points to consider:

1. *The kinds of pictures you will want to take.*
2. *Best size and shape picture for your purpose or liking.*
3. *Convenience in carrying.*

In considering the kinds of subjects you may want to photograph, think also of the range of light conditions under which you may want to take them.

Bear in mind that the lens equipment on a camera has much to do with its versatility.

THE BEST LENS—
WHAT "ANASTIGMAT" MEANS

Unquestionably the finest lens is the anastigmat—the name meaning "without astigmatism." Photographically that means that the picture will be microscopically sharp not only at the central part but from edge to edge of the picture. Negatives with sharply defined images yield clear-cut prints and big enlargements with remarkably fine definition throughout.

The anastigmat offers a further contribution toward quality—it is "faster"—it lets in a greater volume of light than the ordinary lens because it is larger. And the faster the lens the greater the variety of pictures possible. Even for the average amateur the fast lens is decidedly worth while because it lengthens the photo-

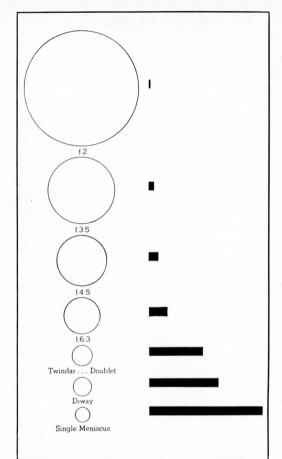

Circles indicate relative speeds. Bars indicate relative times of exposure. The larger (faster) the lens, the shorter the exposure that is needed.

f.2

f.3.5

f.4.5

f.6.3

Twindar . . . Doublet

Diway

Single Meniscus

graphic day. Like the high-powered automobile, it has the speed when you need it.

TYPES OF CAMERAS

For snapshots on very dull gray days, early in the morning or late in the afternoon, for subjects in deep shade, for snapshots indoors, a camera with an *f.*6.3 or faster lens will be of decided advantage. The *f.*6.3 lens is about four times as fast as what is known as a "single" lens such as on most box type cameras, an *f.*4.5 lens is twice as fast as *f.*6.3, the *f.*3.5 is

14

| The Kodak Bantam Special and Retina II have f.2 lenses. | The Kodaks Retina I and Duo Six-20 have f.3.5 lenses. | The Kodak Seniors have f.4.5, f.6.3 and f.11 lenses. | The 3A Kodak, Series II, comes fitted with f.4.5 or f.6.3 lens. |

one and two-thirds times as fast as
$f.4.5$, and the $f.2$ lens is three times
as fast as the $f.3.5$.

SUITABLE SHUTTERS

For general use, even for pictures
of moderately fast-moving objects, a shutter with the 1/100
second speed will fill the bill. It
will be easily seen that to combine
cómpactness with a fast anastigmat lens and suitable shutter
would provide a good, general-
purpose camera. Such a thing
has been done in the Kodak
Seniors and the Kodak Juniors.
Where athletic events or fast
action subjects of any kind are to
be taken, a shutter with greater

*Striking pictures like this are easy with the
fast lens camera. The shafts of sunlight and
silhouetted figures make this forceful, dramatic.*

speeds will be required. There are cameras with $f.4.5$ and even faster
lenses that are equipped with very rapid shutters. For all real speed
work such a combination is necessary, as the fast shutter, when set at full
speed, admits light for only a very small fraction of a second and with
a *slow* lens a satisfactory picture image could not be recorded.

Where compactness and extreme simplicity of operation, combined
with a very fast lens and a high speed shutter, are desired, either a
Kodak Senior or Special with $f.4.5$ lens should be selected. The
Compur Rapid shutter on the Special has a top speed of 1/400 second.   15

Jiffy Kodak has the Twin-
dar, a two-position lens for
near and far subjects.

The Brownies make pic-
tures as close as 5 feet
with their Diway lens.

The Brownie Junior cam-
eras come fitted with the
Single Meniscus lens.

MEI

TWINDAR

f.3.5 AN

JS

. DOUBLET

AN IDEA OF WHAT THE DIFFERENT LENSES CAN DO

The versatility of a camera is governed largely by its optical equipment. The "faster" the lens the greater the variety of pictures that can be taken. The large aperture lens takes clear snapshots under decidedly adverse light conditions. It lengthens the photographic day even into the hours when home lamps are lighted. (See chapter "Snapshots at Night.") Then, too, when extra rapid shutter speeds are required to arrest fast motion the big lens admits sufficient light to record a good picture.

This ability of the faster lenses is best explained graphically. While space does not permit of showing all the types of pictures possible with each lens this grouping indicates the increase in versatility as lens aperture increases.

As designated by the fine line, encompassing each group of pictures, each faster lens has the ability to take all the kinds of pictures in the other groups.

f.6.3 ANASTIGMAT

f.4.5 ANASTIGMAT

IGMAT —— f.2 ANASTIGMAT

RECOMAR: *A versatile, precision built camera for all kinds of pictures. Has f.4.5 lens, takes film packs, cut films, and plates, two sizes, 2¼"x3¼"—3¼"x4¼".*

FOR THE ADVANCED WORKER

An all-'round type of camera for the advanced amateur, considering reasonable compactness, is one with a fast lens, a rapid shutter with a good range of slower automatic speeds, a double extension bellows, for copying and photographing small objects, a graduated distance scale for quick focus, a ground glass panel for focusing and composing a picture in the more exacting work, supplementary lenses for telephoto and wide angle effects, and provision for using various kinds of negative materials.

Such features as these are incorporated in the Kodak Recomar which is equipped with an f.4.5 lens and the Compur shutter.

If compactness is not of prime importance and if much high speed photography will be undertaken in addition to average work, it would be well to consider the Graflex camera, which is made in several sizes. It is equipped with f.4.5 or faster lens, has a great range of shutter timings, especially the higher speeds—up to 1/1000 second. It is constructed to give visual focusing on a ground glass with the image of objects full picture size, right side up, and visible until the moment of tripping the shutter lever to make the exposure.

18

GRAFLEX: *While an ideal camera for speed work it is also suitable for other kinds of pictures. Provides visual focusing up to the instant of exposure.*

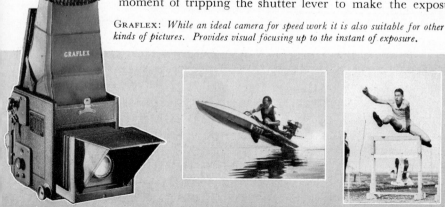

KODAK DUO SIX-20: *A "miniature" for larger pictures . . . sixteen, 1⅝″ x 2¼″, on a roll of No. 620 Film. Shutter speeds to 1/500; lens f.3.5. Negatives yield splendid enlargements.*

EXTREME COMPACTNESS

Where extreme compactness combined with ultra-fast lens is desired, look at the miniature Kodaks—Duo Six-20, Retina, and the Bantam Special, any one of which makes a splendid auxiliary camera to one of larger size. The beautifully designed Bantam Special, and the precision built Retina II are equipped with f.2 lens, Compur-Rapid shutter, speeds to 1/500 second, and a finder that eliminates all guess work in focusing. The Retina and Bantam Special take Kodachrome Color Film as well as film for black and white pictures.

KODAK RETINA II: *Lens f.2 or f.2.8; Shutter 1 to 1/500 second. Eighteen or thirty-six exposures with one loading of "black and white" film and eighteen exposures of Kodachrome.*

Should you want a compact camera that takes larger pictures (2¼ x 3¼ inches or 2½ x 4¼ inches), there is a wide choice of lens equipment, and a wide price range, in the Kodak Juniors and Seniors. Again, if you want box-camera simplicity in an inexpensive, compact folding outfit, examine the Jiffy Kodaks and the Kodak Bantam.

19

KODAK SPECIALS (f.4.5): *Versatile, compact cameras for roll film — picture sizes 2½″ x 4¼″ or 2¼″ x 3¼″. Speeds to 1/400 second, with Compur Rapid shutter.*

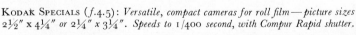

The Bantam, with either *f*.6.3 or Doublet lens, is the smallest of Kodaks, and carries out an entirely new idea in picture making. While it is little bigger than a pack of cigarettes, pictures 2¾ x 4 inches are provided, at small cost, from the diminutive negatives. This has been made possible by special equipment for photo finishers.

MORE ABOUT THE "MINIATURE"

For those who are considering an ultra-fast lens miniature camera either as the one camera for all work or as auxiliary equipment to an outfit that makes larger negatives, these remarks may be of interest.

Features of such an outfit are: Small size, precision construction, an extremely fast, relatively short focus lens, giving greater depth of field than would be optically possible in lenses of similar speed for larger cameras, and an accurate shutter with a wide range of automatic speeds from 1 second to 1/500 second.

Such equipment provides a camera of great versatility. Fast sports shots, pictures under decidedly adverse light conditions outdoors and indoors, even at night and including stage shows, also "off-guard," natural, lifelike shots of unsuspecting children or grown-ups, are all well within the scope of the ultra-fast lens miniature camera. F.4.5 and *f*.6.3 lenses are termed "fast." Lenses rated at *f*.3.5, *f*.2.8, and *f*.2 are considered "ultra-fast." Pictures that heretofore would not have

1/300 *second shutter speed at f*.5.6. *Pan-atomic Film.   Kodak Bantam Special.*

Snapped at f.2 *on Super X Film at* 1/50 *second. Kodak Bantam Special.*

20

Such subjects are now easy with the ultra-fast lens "miniature." This was snapped with a Bantam Special at 1/25 second on Super X Film, lens opening at f.2.

been attempted are easy with these. The exposure required with an *f*.2 lens is, for example, only 1/9 of that needed with an *f*.6.3 lens. Other relative lens speeds are referred to on page 14.

Speed is not the only advantage, however, as ultra-fast miniatures are also very efficient for the carefully planned "still life" or other subject that does not require unusual lens and shutter speed.

Low film cost is a point that appeals to those who take their photography seriously. With low film cost, the enthusiast feels that he can experiment a bit by making a number of exposures of a subject; shots from various angles, with different lightings, filters, and timings, and with different film emulsions. This, to obtain a negative that will give him the "perfect" picture—the one which portrays the subject just as he wishes to show it in an enlargement—perhaps for exhibiting in a salon.

A variety of films is available for the miniature for different kinds of subjects and effects. Kodachrome Film for full color pictures

(transparencies for viewing by projection on a home screen) is available for the Kodaks Retina and Bantam Special.

The pictures on this page and those on pages 20, 21, 92, 148, 153, and 215 give an idea of the miniature Kodak's wide scope and efficiency.

These are all Bantam Special shots on Super X Film.
LEFT: 1/500 *second, at f.*2 *with synchronized Photoflash No.* 20.

ABOVE: 1/50 *second, at f.*2.
LEFT: 1/25 *second, at f.*3.5.

WHAT FILM SHALL I USE AND WHY....

THE answer to this question depends on the kinds of subjects you will be photographing, the type of camera used, the light conditions under which you will work, and, in certain instances, the particular effect you may desire.

You know, of course, that the finest camera in the world would not make fine pictures if it were loaded with inferior film and you no doubt feel that if a picture is worth taking it is worth every effort to secure the best possible results under existing conditions.

The various kinds of film referred to here afford a sufficient choice of emulsions to fill every need of the every-day picture maker. The extent to which photography has advanced is strikingly marked by the newer films.

A GOOD FILM

Kodak Film (Regular) which has been the stand-by of millions of amateurs for over thirty years and has had a steady rise in quality and uniformity during that time, is still available. It has sufficient speed for average use, it is orthochromatic, having high sensitivity to blue, and is somewhat sensitive to green. This film also has good "latitude," that property which allows variations in exposure timings without detriment to negative quality.

Hat, red — *Coat, green* — *Scarf, red, orange, green, brown* — *Skirt, dark blue. The new films record all colors in the relative brightnesses as seen by the eye.*

KODAK "SS" PAN OR
PANATOMIC FILM

FROM ORDINARY FILM
NEGATIVE

"ORTHOCHROMATIC"—WHAT IT MEANS

With a non-orthochromatic film you might be making a picture in which there is a bed of flowers in the foreground—some light yellow blooms, others dark blue and, of course, with green foliage. The negative would yield a print in which the yellow flowers would appear darker than the blue ones, though to the eye yellow is lighter. The green foliage would also appear darker than it did to the eye.

In other words, the film would not give true color values. The fully orthochromatic film corrects these mistakes and renders the color *values* (intensities of color brightnesses) in their proper relation to each other in the black and white print. It is not, however, sensitive to red as is panchromatic film.

Color values may be further accentuated by the use of the proper color filters. See chapter on filters, page 84.

24

Made on Kodak "SS" Pan Film. Light, hazy; ½ second, stop f.45.

Note, in the two lower pictures, the freedom from halation ("fuzziness" or spreading of light around bright lights). Notice also the improvement in color value renderings, especially in the bottom picture.

KODAK VERICHROME FILM

FOR day in and day out picture making there is nothing better. Verichrome Film has proved its superiority to snapshooter and advanced worker alike. It is a fast film, with sufficient speed to permit of making snapshots on days when the sun is not shining brightly. In addition to good speed it has other properties that make it a favorite all-season film. Verichrome is highly orthochromatic.

KODAK FILM (REGULAR)

In landscapes, for example, it preserves excellent tone values of the bright yellows, the browns, and greens of the woods and fields which on a "color blind" film would photograph almost uniformly dark. Verichrome "picks up" shadow detail, and bright highlights will not "block up." These qualities also make it an ideal negative material for the snow scenic.

Its long tone scale, that records detail in shadows as well as highlights, provides the property needed for natural, lifelike pictures of people. Without this gradation, such pictures would be too harsh and "contrasty," especially when taken in brilliant sunlight which casts heavy shadows.

KODAK VERICHROME FILM

DOUBLE-COATED

Verichrome is a *double-coated* film; this unique feature gives it special properties—among them, extraordinary latitude.

PROTECTION AGAINST HALATION

A further advantage of Verichrome is secured by a dye on the back of the film (which disappears in

25

KODAK "SS" PAN FILM

"Westward"   *Good geometric design nicely spaced within the picture area.
Fine balance of tone masses; "action," forward motion of the
boat is at once sensed. Tonal qualities were splendidly recorded on the Verichrome Film negative. 1/100 second, stop f.22.
fairly low sun in front, to the right, just out of the lens angle.*

A *First coating prevents this weak, washed-out effect, by correcting OVERexposure* (LEFT).

B *Second coating prevents this blackish, sooty effect, by helping to prevent UNDERexposure. The two coatings combined, one slow and one fast, assure proper exposure throughout the picture and give you this clear, crisp snapshot, rich in detail* (RIGHT).

developing). This colored backing controls "halation"—the spreading of light from a bright object—to a considerable degree, making possible clearer-cut pictures of subjects in brilliant sunlight and of night illuminations, as shown on page 25. The non-halation property is also valuable for indoor studies when a sunlighted window comes within the picture setting.

Verichrome will pick up that elusive shadow detail in snow pictures. (LEFT)

No longer need your subjects face into the glaring sunlight. (RIGHT)

KODAK "SS" PAN FILM

A SUPERIOR FILM, Kodak Super Sensitive Panchromatic provides all users of roll-film and film-pack cameras with the advantages of great speed and *complete* color sensitivity heretofore available only in cut film and plates.

With fast lens equipment snapshots like this are possible.

The extreme speed of Kodak "SS" Pan Film makes possible snapshots indoors by artificial light, thus extending the snapshot day into the hours when lamps are lighted.

Lifelike, unposed, informal home pictures of the family, even of the lively youngsters with their pets, can now be caught in a fraction of a second, and at night by replacing a few of the regular bulbs in the lamps with Mazda Photoflood bulbs and loading with "SS" Film. With No. 2 Photofloods, snapshots may be made indoors even with box type cameras if loaded with "SS" Film. Snapshots of your city's illuminated shopping and theater districts, too, are easy with this film and an $f.6.3$ or faster lens; and with ultra-fast lenses ($f.3.5—f.2$), bits of brightly lighted stage shows and indoor athletic events can be recorded.

Superior scenic pictures like these two are easy with "SS" Pan Film and color filters.

ITS EXTRA SPEED

Because of its unusual sensitivity to orange and red, Kodak Super Sensitive Panchromatic Film is considerably faster than ordinary film by artificial light. Its speed is not noticeably greater than that of ordinary film in midday sun but is definitely greater by early morning and late afternoon light. "SS" Pan has a relatively high sensitivity to green and renders its brightness much as received by the eye.

28

DOUBLE-COATED ... NON-HALATION

Like Verichrome, Kodak "SS" Pan Film has two coatings of light-sensitive silver. The supersensitive coating catches detail in dark parts of the subject, thus guarding against *under*exposure. Beneath it is a slow coating, to retain detail in bright parts and guard against *over*exposure.

Whether pictures are made in daytime or at night, the non-halation quality is of great value.

SUPERIOR FOR DAYLIGHT PICTURES

By daylight as well as by electric light, the complete color sensitivity of the film, in addition to its extreme speed, is of decided advantage. A film sensitive to *all* colors records hues of nature, colors of clothing, and flesh tones more in the brightnesses as seen by the eye. The result is that prints in black and white are more beautiful and realistic than those made from a negative material not completely color-sensitive, and they are especially suitable for coloring.

Full-toned, well-timed pictures are obtained in the soft yellow light of the very early hours of morning and the late hours of afternoon—the times of day when long shadows so richly enhance pictorial studies. Renderings are further improved by the use of the proper color filters. Information on filters and filter factors is given with the film and on page 84.

KODAK SUPER X PANCHROMATIC FILM

Super X is an exceptionally fast film for Kodaks Retina and Bantam, also the Leica, Contax and similar cameras. It goes a step further even than "SS" Pan. Given proper development, it exhibits greater speed—in daylight as well as in artificial light. It affords assurance of properly timed negatives where fast shutter actions are required and is ideal for night photography with artificial light.

29

Snapshots like these two, in-doors, at night, can now be made with "SS" Pan and Photofloods.

Fully timed outdoor action "shots" at high shutter speeds can now be made earlier in morning or later in afternoon.

KODAK PANATOMIC FILM

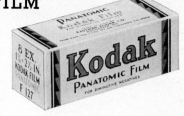

Every photographic film has grain—but that of Panatomic Film is of almost atomic fineness. This means that when a picture is enlarged to many times its size, the grain is still so fine that remarkable sharpness and brilliance, and much of the contact print quality, are retained. If you use a miniature camera you will find that Panatomic Film will yield strikingly beautiful enlargements. And its fine grain is just as valuable when bigger negatives are to be greatly enlarged, though splendid enlargements may be secured from other Kodak Films. It is a double-coated film and like Super Sensitive Panchromatic has a tinted backing which greatly aids in the prevention of halation.

Panatomic has almost the same speed as Verichrome Film to daylight and for average daylight the same exposure is recommended; its sensitivity to yellow, red, and green yields fully-timed negatives earlier or later in the day than non-panchromatic film.

Its high sensitivity to artificial light makes it ideal for night photography, when fine grain negative material is required. As will be seen in the table below on comparative film speeds it is somewhat faster than Verichrome under artificial light. Kodak Panatomic Film is *completely* color-sensitive—"panchromatic" and may be obtained in rolls, packs, and cut sheets.

COMPARATIVE SPEEDS OF KODAK FILMS*		
Material	Speed	
	Daylight	Photoflood Lamps
Kodak Film (Regular)............	120	40
Kodak Verichrome Film...........	180	80
Kodak "SS" Panchromatic Film.....	240	160
Kodak Super X Panchromatic Film...	320	210
Kodak Panatomic Film...........	160†	100†

*Figures obtained by a standard system of speed evaluation employed in the Kodak Research Laboratories.

†When developed in the Elon-Hydroquinone-Borax Developer, Formula D-76.

These pictures made on Infra-Red negative material are not what they seem. The winter "night" shot was made late in the afternoon, the wintry looking landscape at the right was made in the summer. Note recording of distant detail.

KODAK INFRA-RED FILM

FOR AMATEUR USE

This film reaches into that portion of the spectrum beyond the visible red. It is especially useful in long distance photography because of its ability to cut out haze. An infra-red photograph taken with a deep red or a deep yellow filter will often render distant objects clearly, even if the haze makes them invisible to the eye. Photographs taken by infra-red, outdoors in sunlight, have the appearance of pictures taken by moonlight. Wratten Filters Nos. 15 (G), 25 (A), 70, 88-A and 89-A can be used with practically the same results and the same filter factor. Average exposure time, under normal conditions for landscapes, 1/25 second with stop $f.4.5$ with filter. For high contrast develop in D-19; for low contrast in D-76. The Infra-Red Film is available only in the No. I-R 135 Kodak Film Magazine for use in the Kodak Retina, and the Leica, Contax and similar cameras; this emulsion is also obtainable on glass plates.

KODACHROME

FOR FULL-COLOR PICTURES
WITH MINIATURE CAMERAS

This unique full color film that has created such a sensation among home movie fans is available for certain miniature "still" cameras. It is spooled for the Kodak Bantam Special, the Kodak Retina and similar cameras. Kodachrome provides gorgeous, pure color transparencies with the ease of ordinary black and white snapshots. No extra equipment is required for the average "shots." The color is in the film. The full color transparencies can either be viewed in their original size or projected in enlarged form on a screen. Materials for assembling slides, and the Kodaslide Projector are available at Kodak dealer's. The original price of the film includes processing in the Kodak laboratories. Black and white prints and color prints can be made from Kodachrome transparencies. Printed directions may be obtained through your dealer or by writing direct to Eastman Kodak Company, Rochester, N. Y.

The full, natural colors of scenes like this may now be recorded easily with Kodachrome.

From a Kodachrome transparency.
Made with one No. 10 Photoflash in a Kodak Handy Reflector at six feet from subject.
Diaphragm opening f.8; Type A Kodachrome Film.

From a Kodachrome transparency.
Made at 1/250 second, diaphragm opening f.3.5.

A FEW CONCISE
POINTERS
FOR THE
BEGINNER

Assuming that you have learned the operation of your camera—from the manual that came with it—there are but three things to remember for securing good results.

(1) Correct focus to assure sharp, distinct images; (2) Proper exposure to yield a technically good negative that will in turn give a clear print; (3) Good composition which makes the picture pleasing.

These three points are the basis of good picture making; master them and you'll soon be an expert. The following simplified general directions should prove helpful to your progress.

IF YOUR CAMERA IS OF THE FOLDING TYPE

To get nearby objects (6 to 15 feet away) sharp with a focusing camera, pace off the distance, knowing the length of your stride, or better still use the Kodak Pocket Range Finder, then set the pointer at the right mark. Distances of 25 feet or more may be safely estimated, but if you are not a good "guesser," measure anything less or use the Range Finder (see page 37).

For proper exposures of different types of subjects and under various light conditions, it is best at first to refer to the exposure tables in your camera manual or to the one on page 54 of this book. Once you acquire the knack of judging the light and of setting the shutter speed and stop opening properly, you can readily gauge the exposure correctly—under like conditions—the next time. Experience and observation

Tipping the camera sideways even makes boats sail downhill, as in picture at right. Hold the camera level unless you're trying for an unusual effect.

When one's eyeglasses are misty things cannot be seen distinctly. Just so with the camera's eye ... keep the lens clean for clear, bright pictures.

The camera doesn't have an "X-ray" eye; it cannot see through even a tip of a finger. Picture at right shows result of a finger in front of lens.

With focusing cameras be sure to set the lens at the correct distance mark. The blurred picture at right is "out of focus." Focus was incorrectly set for distance between subject and lens.

Two other causes of blurred pictures are: Camera was moved when shutter was clicked or shutter speed was not rapid enough to "stop" the action. The latter accounts for the "fuzzy" snapshot at the right.

On this and on the following page are shown common mistakes that spoil good pictures. Fine pictures on the left, spoiled pictures on the right! Study them, read the explanations, and guard your pictures from these mistakes.

(right). Shutter speed not fast enough to arrest action from broadside position. Such moving objects can be caught, even with an ordinary camera, if taken from an angle and not too close up, as at left.

Two pictures are spoiled when you forget to turn the film and a "double" exposure is made on one section. Acquire the habit of always turning to the next number immediately after you've made a picture.

Poorly chosen backgrounds, especially for informal portraits, often mar an otherwise good picture. How much better the picture on the left than the one on the right. Choose your background setting carefully.

teach much in this most fascinating hobby—amateur picture making.

While it is probably better for the beginner that his subject be lighted from the front or side, he can make unusually attractive pictures "against" the light.

After a little experience, try a few "shots" of this kind, with the sunlight well to the side or even in back of the subject, but be careful to shade the lens so that direct sunlight does not strike into it as this would fog and blur the picture. For further details on "back-lighted" pictures see pages 67, 68, and observe those throughout this volume where the subjects are lighted from the rear or from well to the side.

Study the picture image in the finder; what you see there you will get in the picture. Select a viewpoint from which the subject appears properly lighted and from which uninteresting or distracting objects are not visible.

Good likenesses in outdoor informal portraits are best made when the subject does not face into the sun. Better have the strong light coming well from one side, as in the picture on the left, then time the exposure to record detail in the shaded side of the face.

The picture on the right, of the same young lady, was taken at noon out in the glaring sun. *With the sun high in the sky deep shadows are cast in the eyes and from the nose making a good likeness impossible. When taking pictures of people, around the noon hours especially, have them in the shade just out of the sunlight area. Snapshots can be made in the shade with the new, fast Kodak Films.*

IF YOU HAVE A BOX CAMERA

With the ordinary box camera that has no special adjustment for nearby and distant objects all objects farther than eight or ten feet will appear reasonably sharp. The manual that came with the camera tells how far you must be away from a subject to get a sharp image with it.

Since simplicity is the keynote, the box camera naturally has less range of performance than one of the folding type on which the lens can be adjusted or focused for objects at various distances. However, the Six-16 and Six-20 Brownies, with their Diway lens, have a "two-point" focus feature and objects as close up as five feet can be taken as well as distant objects. With the box camera and ordinary film,

If you tip the camera up very much when taking a building the result will be like this. The lines converge toward the top and the building appears to be leaning backward. Better back off a bit to get the top in rather than tip camera for such subjects.

snapshots should be made only in bright sunlight, though with Kodak Verichrome Film satisfactory results can be obtained in the open or "bright" shade and on days of hazy sunshine.

Except with this film, "SS" Pan, or Panatomic, do not make snapshots with box cameras in early morning or late afternoon ("SS" Pan and Panatomic are of greatest help at such times). The sun may appear to be bright, but its light is not strong at these hours as it is filtered through much of the earth's surface haze. Use a large stop, generally, for snapshots of nearby subjects, a smaller stop for distant views. The exposure table on page 54 shows just how to set the camera for all kinds of outdoor subjects. For indoor pictures, see page 125.

BEFORE YOU CLICK THE SHUTTER

When you are about to snap the picture, hold the camera steady, and locate the image in the finder as you would like it to appear in the resulting picture. Be sure that the film has been turned to a new section if you have previously been making pictures.

Hold the camera level. For photographs of buildings or objects where there are prominent vertical lines this is especially important. As you progress, however, you will find that splendid pictures of certain subjects, and interesting odd angle effects, can be made by pointing the camera up or down as described on pages 69 to 71.

RANGE FINDER TAKES GUESSWORK OUT OF FOCUSING

The Kodak Pocket Range Finder eliminates all guesswork in focusing. The correct distance is read directly while viewing the subject. The illustration shows just how the finder works.

It is especially valuable when fast lenses are used at their wide apertures with the accompanying lack of depth of field.

Kodak Pocket Range Finder is small, and may be clipped in a vest pocket.

At the correct distance there is no break in the image above and below the horizontal line (right). Note the scale at the left, read while viewing the subject.

"Long Legs"

To see good picture subjects in commonplace things is essential if you would acquire a collection of really fine photographs. Some of the best pictures in salons are of subjects that just "happened" but were recognized by an alert camera fan. Without the shadows this picture would not have been nearly so effective.

Also had one or more of the boys been looking toward the camera the spontaneity and story-telling qualities would have been considerably weakened. Note the expressions; they were probably inspired by something the photographer said. This back-lighted picture was made with a Kodak Recomar on "SS" Pan Film, 1/100 second, lens opening at f.8.

AN INTERESTING AND INSTRUCTIVE EXPERIMENT

See How the Lens Forms the Picture Image • See Just What Happens When You Do Not Focus Correctly • See What Effect "Stopping Down" the Lens Has on the Picture.

An interesting experiment easily performed will give a very good idea of just what happens when the various adjustments are made, such as focusing and changing the diaphragm stop.

Remove the back of the camera and look through the lens towards the sky or any bright object. Set the shutter on "Time" and operate it. Note how it opens when the lever or cable release is pressed, and closes again on the next pressure. Set it on "B" and operate it again, noting how this differs from "T" or "Time." Then try the different speed settings.

Again, set the shutter on "Time" and open it, then operate the iris diaphragm and note how it opens and closes, making the opening larger or smaller.

Now to see how images are formed on the film, place the camera (with the back off) on a table pointing it out of a window towards some object such as a house or tree. If the

First step in carrying on the experiment described.

39

camera is 6 feet back from the window it will help in carrying out part of the experiment.

Next, place a small piece of ground glass over the opening at the back of the camera where the film ordinarily lies. The ground side of the glass should be toward the lens. If ground glass is not available, a piece of tissue paper can be stretched across the back of the camera, although this does not give as clear an image as does ground glass.

AN UPSIDE DOWN PICTURE

With the shutter open and the focusing scale set at 100 feet, an image of the outside object will be seen. If you have never tried the experiment before, you will perhaps be surprised to find that the image is upside down. The inverted image is a natural consequence of the manner in which a lens transmits the rays of light that pass through it to form the picture image. This is a fundamental law of optics, though it does not matter in the least because when we finally receive the picture we naturally look at it right side up.

"STOPPING DOWN"

To continue the experiment, change the diaphragm setting from a large opening to a small one while watching the image on the ground glass. Note how the image changes in brightness as the stop opening is changed.

FOCUSING

One of the most important adjustments on the camera is the focusing device. To see how this works, change the distance setting through as large a range as possible while watching the image at the back of the camera. Note that there is one certain setting at which the image is especially sharp and clear. At other distance settings it is more or less blurred and indistinct so that fine detail can not be seen.

Now having secured a sharp image of the outside object, without changing the focus, observe the image of some nearer object, say at 6 feet from the lens.

THE "OUT-OF-FOCUS" IMAGE

If the camera is pointed out of a window at this distance, a vase of flowers on the window sill will serve as an excellent near object. The image of such a nearby object will appear blurred if the lens is set for distant objects. If the focusing adjustment is changed, a setting can be found which will give a sharp image of the flowers, but the image of the distant object will then be blurred. Trying this experiment will more quickly convince one of the necessity of accurate focusing for the object of interest than many pages of discussion of the matter. The focusing experiment should be tried both with the largest and the smaller stops, when it will be found that if a *small* stop opening is used it is possible to have both near and far objects reasonably sharp at the same time. This shows us the reason why a simple box camera has no elaborate focusing equipment—it has a lens with a small stop.

If there is much light in the room in which this interesting experiment is being carried on it may be difficult to see the image on the ground glass, especially when using a small stop. In such a case, use a black cloth around the back of the camera and over the head to exclude stray light, being careful that the cloth does not get in front of the lens. With this arrangement the experiment can be tried out-of-doors if desired.

NOTES

(A) When looking for the image on the ground glass, remember that the image is *on* the ground glass, so the eyes must be kept 10 inches or so away. Look *at* the ground glass, not through it.

(B) With lenses on some of the very inexpensive cameras the best image of a distant object may be obtained on the ground glass when the focusing scale is not quite at the 100 foot mark. If such a discrepancy is found, it does not mean that the focusing scale is in error. It is merely evidence that the lens is of a type that has a small amount of "chromatic aberration." The light to which the eye is most sensitive does not come to the same focus as that to which the film is most sensitive, consequently the *visual* image may not be quite at its best with the lens focused for 100 feet. The only real check on the markings of the focusing scale with such lenses is the taking of pictures.

CHILDREN

HOW TO MAKE NATURAL, APPEALING PICTURES OF THEM

IF YOU are a parent no group of prints in the album will ever be treasured more than those representing the picture biography of your children. As these are such important pictures you will probably welcome some hints on how to get best results.

First, let us suggest that you keep a chronological Kodak story of the growth of the child—an intimate picture diary from cradle days up through college years.

Begin by making a few pictures each week; thus every change in the child will be permanently recorded in prints you will enjoy now and cherish in later years. Children *will* grow up, but you can keep them just as they are, forever—in pictures.

SOME HIGHLIGHTS IN A KODAK BIOGRAPHY

To make the picture biography of most value, it is well to acquire the knack of making interesting pictures, and the following subject suggestions may be a help to this end. There will, of course, be many other opportunities; pictures that will fall into their natural sequence in the album.

DON'T POSE THEM

Avoid pictures that appear to have been carefully posed. This is especially important in obtaining appealing little studies of the youngsters. Guard against too many "see-the-birdie" expressions. The truly interesting pictures show no evidence of having been posed. To make such pictures of children we must snap them as they really are—natural, unaffected, carefree. Those who are experienced know the advantage of inventing or seizing upon situations in which children are really interested. It is usually a bit difficult for little people to make believe under observation or with a camera pointed at them, and it is easier for

43

SPECIAL PICTURE OCCASIONS

"One Day Old" Shots.

Series of infant pictures, made weekly.

His "Majesty's" or Her "Highness'" initial ride in the carriage.

The bath (good for a special series through the early years).

First steps, important pictures indeed.

Playroom studies—chances galore (see page 120).

Nap time, see page 115.

Dinner time, see page 117.

From baby dresses to child clothes.

With mother.

The first family snapshot— with dad and mother.

With the grandparents.

With favorite doll or toy.

Playing with a pet.

A series of story-telling pictures around a main idea. See pages 46, 50.

Each birthday—a momentous occasion (perhaps with the ceremonial cake and its candles which date the picture).

Now to face the world— off to school.

First attempt on skates.

Tea party on the lawn.

The birthday party picture.

Vacation activities.

At scout age—boy or girl.

High school or "Prep"— another milestone.

College years.

44

them to make the necessary concessions about any slight change of position when they are interested in the "stage setting" or "properties." Favorite toys, books, and pets will help to hold attention and give point to the picture.

You should, of course, try to record the spontaneous action, look, or gesture. Pictorially, such snapshots have an appeal all their own. The important thing is that the picture should look natural whether it has been planned or just happened.

WITH THE PETS

Children with pets are naturally so charming that it is best to let them pose themselves. Simply watch the play and take a series of pictures without making an important issue of the occasion. After a few incidents have been pictured you can perhaps make one or two closeup— something possibly a little more formal. When you do want a picture of the child looking toward the camera, don't wait long to "click" it, for if you do a self-conscious expression may creep in. Get him interested in something and when you are all ready, attract his attention— then snap promptly. Another scheme is to have someone near you do something that is likely to bring the desired expression. Note the many such pictures in this volume.

When photographing small children who are sitting or playing on the ground or floor it is best to stoop and hold the camera in a lower position than would be the case if taking a picture of a grown-up. This method is generally better than tilting the camera downward, though there will be times when striking and unusual pictures can be made from the higher angle. There are references to camera angles on page 69.

Where you wish to point the camera downward a trifle be sure that there are no prominent vertical lines in objects within the picture area, as tilting the camera will give a convergence of such lines in the re-

Shadows make this interesting. A 1/10 second exposure at f.8. Sunlight entering large window at right.

One, two
  Buckle my shoe.
Three, four
  Close the door.
Five, six
  Pick up sticks.
Seven, eight
  Lay them straight.
Nine, ten
  A big fat hen.

Many nursery rimes are excellent vehicles for a series of story-telling pictures.

sulting picture. With low camera position, however, you will more clearly see the features of your subjects. The infant who is too small to sit up can be "snapped" in his mother's arms, in his carriage, or placed between pillows in a rounded back chair. Comfortably placed in such positions he will be anything but a difficult subject.

THOSE FIRST TODDLING STEPS

A few pictures of the child who is just learning to walk are indeed high spots in any Kodak biography. Such pictures can be made with the child toddling away from the camera as well as toward it and the two views make an appealing combination on the album page. There is a little trick in getting a sharp image of any moving object, especially

46

when it is reasonably near the camera. When using the focusing type of camera, decide at just what distance you will take the picture—perhaps six or eight feet. Set the focus for the distance chosen, pace it off on the sidewalk or lawn and *mark* the position in some manner, possibly with a twig or bit of paper. Then have someone start the child off toward you and when he reaches the marked position, press the shutter lever. Of course, with the ordinary box type camera the image would be reasonably sharp if the child is

A "First Steps" Picture.

eight or ten feet away but not closer, except when making close-ups with a Kodak Portrait Attachment over the lens (see page 112). With the Six-16 and Six-20 Brownies subjects can be photographed about five feet away without a portrait attachment.

The attractive "off to school" picture at the bottom of page 44 is another interesting story-telling situation that should not be overlooked. Here the children may have to do a bit of easy acting, but if you do not fuss much you will get a natural and apparently unstudied picture for the "growing up" collection.

The Kodak Self Timer, for any camera with cable release, or the built-in self timer on certain Kodaks, permits you to get into the family group snapshot.

First Family Snapshot; at 2 months.

These are but high spots in the picture biography of a boy. Here, he is shown from the babe-in-arms age to eighteen. Such a picture history is fun in the making and increases greatly in interest and in value with the years. Let your Kodak be family historian.

Two Years; "Taking Things Apart" Age.

His First Circus Where He Tried Out His First Camera

Vacation Days, When He Was 11.

12 Years; With "Good Old" Rex.

Carriage Days; 6 months.

First
Birthday;
Every
Birthday
a Picture
Occasion.

3 Years; "Knee Deep in June."

The Fifth
Winter . . .
and a
New Sled.

10 Years;
an "Off to
School" Shot.

The Day of Days
His Seventh.

Scouting
Days;
He's 13
here.

That Summer at Camp;
He was 15 then.

Girl Interest at 18.

MAKE A SERIES OF PICTURES HAVING "CONTINUITY"

This splendid plan of making a series of story-telling pictures around a central idea is well worth the attention of every parent. There are numbers of nursery rimes that can be used as a basis for special groups of pictures.

What a charming series of pictures you could make illustrating the "Five Senses"—Seeing, Smelling, Tasting, Feeling, and Hearing. The pictures here and on page 46 show something of what can be accomplished. You will also find pictures of children in costume particularly appealing; and what youngster doesn't like to "dress up"?

THE KODAK SELF TIMER

The Self Timer may be used with any camera that has a cable release to operate the shutter. It automatically "presses the button" in from one-half second to one minute after being set. Just set the Timer for the interval desired and then everyone can get into the picture, making the group complete. The Timer likewise permits of self portraiture. Certain Kodaks have a self-timing device incorporated in their shutters. The Optipod is also a clever device which holds the Kodak and clamps to table edge, shelf, window ledge, or running board of the car, and with its ball and socket joint permits tilting the camera

SEEING

SMELLING

TASTING

FEELING

HEARING

at almost any angle. The Kodapod, another accessory, holds the Kodak clamped to tree, stick, bench, or fence.

LET YOUR KODAK BE FAMILY HISTORIAN

The Optipod   *Kodapod and Self Timer*

Mother, dad, brother Bill, and sister Sue as well as other members of the family should be represented in the household picture album, in separate intimate, natural snapshots. Together with informal portraits made amid the home atmosphere you'll want many story-telling pictures. There's Uncle Ed sprawled on the floor with Bill and Sue, putting together that big jig-saw map—surely a picture chance. Then be ready when dad dozes off for his "forty winks" in the over-stuffed chair after Sunday dinner.

Wander out into the kitchen with the Kodak—there's mother putting the finishing touches on a luscious frosted cake, or Amelia, the cook, "basting" a well-browned turkey. Photoflash makes such shots easy.

Upstairs, Aunt Lou is writing to—well, she won't tell—but anyhow she makes a pretty picture with pen poised at her new Queen Anne desk. (For indoor picture instructions see page 106.) Later on, glancing out of the window you spy Grandad pushing Billy about in the old wheelbarrow—quick! don't miss it—they're *both* youngsters now!

There are chances every day to record the home story in pictures.

51

A Self Timer "Shot," half second, stop f.6.3.

EXPOSURES FOR OUTDOOR PICTURES

Exposure—on that and development depends the technical quality of your pictures. Expert finishers will take care of the latter, if you do not care to do your own, but you must assume responsibility for the former.

If there were but one correct exposure for a certain type of subject at a certain hour of a certain month, with sunlight, there would indeed be a complex problem to solve when exposures were to be made at other times, but there is no such problem because there are *several* exposures, each of which will prove correct for various kinds of subjects during several hours of every day in the year. Too, the introduction of Verichrome and other fast Kodak Films with their remarkable latitude has greatly simplified things. As previously mentioned, "latitude" is that property in a film which allows variation in exposure without detriment to negative quality.

Exposure 1/25 second, stop f.22. Shadow detail in foreground figure and tree was not desired.

52

FOUR SUBJECT GROUPS

By listing in four groups (see page 54), the kinds of subjects that are most popular and adopting as a standard exposure for each group one that is intermediate between the shortest and longest time that will yield a satisfactory negative, there will be only *four* exposures to consider with any given type of camera.

With double lens cameras the same shutter speed can be used, with different stops, for each group. With single lens cameras the same shutter speed can likewise be used for three of the groups and a time exposure given for subjects in the fourth. The pictures on pages 55 to 57 are designated as to the groups in which they belong. They serve as a guide to acquaint you with the exposures required for different kinds of subjects.

THE FASTER LENSES

With cameras that have *f*.6.3 or faster lenses good negatives can be obtained under decidedly adverse light conditions, when the lens is used at its full opening. For general subjects such as listed, however, and with the light conditions good, there is no need to use larger stop openings than those given in the table.

The advantage of using the smaller openings in the lens ("stopping down" it is called) is that a greater range of sharpness is secured in objects at various distances from the camera. This, of course, is desirable in most pictures and is known as an increase in *depth of field*.

53

A DEPENDABLE OUTDOOR EXPOSURE TABLE *

These exposures are for 1 hour after sunrise until 1 hour before sunset with Verichrome, "SS" Pan, and Panatomic Films. With Kodak Film (Regular) the exposures given are for 2½ hours after sunrise until 2½ hours before sunset.	For folding camera with double lens			For folding camera with single lens		For the Jiffy Kodaks with Twindar Lens and fixed focus box camera with doublet lens and three stops	For the Jiffy Kodak V. P. with doublet lens and fixed focus box cameras with single and Diway lenses and two stops	For fixed focus box camera with single lens and three stops
	Shutter Speed	Stops marked in f. System	Stops marked in Uniform System	Shutter Speed	Stop			
GROUP 1—Marine and Beach Scenes—Distant Landscapes—Snow without Prominent Dark Objects in the Foreground.....	1/25	(f.) 22	U. S. 32	1/25	3	Snapshot with Smallest Stop	Snapshot with Small Stop	Snapshot with Middle Stop
GROUP 2 — Ordinary Landscapes with Sky, with Principal Object in the Foreground......	1/25	16	16	1/25	2	Snapshot with Middle Stop	Snapshot with Large Stop	Snapshot with Largest Stop
GROUP 3—Near-by Landscapes Showing Little or No Sky — Groups, Street Scenes.........	1/25	11	8	1/25	1	Snapshot with Largest Stop	Snapshot with Large Stop	Snapshot with Largest Stop
GROUP 4—Portraits in the Open Shade (not under trees or the roof of a porch)—Shaded Near-by Scenes...............	1/25	7.7 7.9 or 8	4	1 sec.	3	1 second with Smallest Stop	1 second with Small Stop	1 second with Smallest Stop

The table above is for exposures when the sun is shining. When the day is cloudy the exposures should be about twice as long, and when very dull, about four times as long. Steady the camera against the body and hold the breath for the instant, when making snapshots. Rest the camera on a solid support for time exposures.

*The "Miniatures": Unless camera is on a rigid support it is best, with the fast miniature Kodaks, to use the 1/50 or 1/100 shutter speeds to prevent image blur from slight camera movement. Settings for average subjects would be 1/50 at f.8 or 1/100 at f.5.6. Special tables are included in manuals with the miniatures.

Some subjects that belong in Group 1.

The shortest possible "time" exposure is of vastly longer duration than the slowest snapshot that most cameras will make. Therefore the lens should always be stopped down for an outdoor time exposure.

MOVING OBJECTS

While all of the combinations of stops and shutter speeds that are recommended in the table are eminently satisfactory for photographing stationary objects, all of them are not adapted for photographing rapidly moving objects.

It is obvious that sharp images of moving objects can only be secured with quick shutter actions. A good rule, when using the average hand camera for picturing anything that is moving rapidly, is to use the largest stop and give the shortest exposure that the shutter can make. The subject must, of course, be in sunlight. In this we are of course referring to ordinary cameras, not the cameras with ultra-fast lenses.

Some subjects that belong in Group 2. 55

Some subjects that belong in Group 3.

Blur from movement of subject naturally becomes less apparent in the picture as the distance between the subject and the camera is increased. Rapid action can be arrested more easily as the angle at which the object comes toward the camera or moves away from it becomes more acute. To illustrate: If a moderately fast moving object is traveling at right angles to the camera at a speed of say ten miles an hour it should be photographed at a distance of seventy-five feet with the ordinary camera. If it is moving diagonally across the field of view it may be photo-

It would be best to class a winter's scene of this kind in Group 3.

56

A summer scenic of this kind might well be classed in Group 2.

graphed at a distance of fifty feet, while if it is moving directly toward or away from the camera it can be photographed at a distance of about thirty feet, with the assurance of equally sharp images of the object being obtained in each case.

The most pleasing pictures of moving objects are usually obtained when the subject is moving diagonally across the field of view at somewhere near a 45° angle, and it is comparatively easy to arrest the motion from such a viewpoint. When necessary to take action subjects at a distance bigger images may be obtained by enlarging. You can readily see, on the easel, just how far you can "blow" the image up before objectionable blur from any unarrested movement shows.

Some subjects that belong in Group 4.   **57**

HOW TO MAKE PICTURES INTERESTING

If you have your snapshots "say something" they will have general appeal and will "live" longer. Have you ever had an enthusiast hand you a collection of prints which, while good technically, did not particularly interest you? Next time this fellow reaches for his latest efforts you will probably groan inwardly.

Why your indifference? The answer, no doubt, is that the prints are nearly all pictures with no particular point to them, no story value, no apparent reason for having been made. They are merely

LEFT: *Excellent composition. Had the boy or man faced the camera the interest would have been divided.*

AT BOTTOM, OPPOSITE PAGE: *This scenic with figures could be divided in half but is still interesting in its entirety.*

photographic records of one or more persons, probably with self-conscious expressions, staring at the camera. Pictures of the same subjects would have held your attention, if there had been an idea behind them.

True it is, however, that at times you will want a few informal little Kodak portraits, or close-ups of members of the family or friends—pictures made in the home surroundings. These are in a class by themselves, and are easily recognized and valued as such.

Even so, it is often possible to introduce some accessory that will tend to relieve an otherwise stiff or awkward pose. You will want a good likeness when you make a picture of a person, and you want the subject to appear natural and the position or attitude unstudied. A book for dad, a doll for little Madge, sister at the piano, mother at the tulip bed, Junior with the pup, are simply suggestions.

In such pictures, where a good likeness is more important than the story-telling element, the subject may (or may not) look directly at the camera, and the person need not necessarily be busily engrossed with the so-called accessory—it is of secondary importance.

A few adults and some children can stand before the camera for more than a second or two and not appear or feel self-conscious. With such subjects, there is no need for including anything to help give them poise. Bear in mind, however, that, in all pictures of people they should at least look happy or interested.

So much in explanation for those who say, "What about 'close-ups' or portraits?"

And now for other pictures of the story-telling variety. In the first place it is seldom that such a picture can be made with the subject looking directly at the camera. He should be engaged in some sort of

AT TOP: *A charming child study "caught" at just the right moment.*

CENTER: *The album, as an accessory, provides a point of interest.*

BOTTOM: *Another natural child picture. Note that she is not looking at the camera.*

The house in the lower right nicely balances the composition and accentuates the height of the mountains. Made on Panatomic Film, K-1 Filter, 1/25 second f.16.

activity or pastime, seemingly unaware of the presence of the camera.

Look over the pictures in this book and you will clearly see what is meant. Though you may not even know the people, most of these pictures are probably interesting to you because they tell some little story and tell it at a glance.

Making a picture tell a story is by no means difficult. It may require just a little thought on your part and some cooperation from your subjects, though there will be times when you can "catch" them unaware in an unposed story-telling situation. Then you will have made an honest-to-goodness story-telling picture.

There are story-telling situations on every hike, on every picnic, auto trip, or wherever children play. The particular kinds of pictures to which your attention is directed are those of everyday incidents, either about the home or away from it.

You can make pictures in which you are included if your shutter has a self-timer adjustment; or by employing the Kodak Self Timer on the cable release of shutters so equipped.

In any event, whether taking pictures of yourself, children, or friends, make the Kodak tell a story. As time goes on you will find yourself making that kind above all others, and friends will give much more than a polite glance at them.

Of course, the beautiful landscape or marine subject will tell its own story, but how it tells it will depend on the point of view from which you take the picture. Here is where a bit of knowledge about composition comes in handy—see page 62. Such pictures can be made with or with-

Costume pictures are alluring.

out human figures, but if persons are included they should not be too prominent nor should they be looking toward the camera lens—give nature a chance to express itself. (See pages 80, 81.)

Your cleverness in making pictures *interesting* will, of course, be reflected in the prints and enlargements from your negatives. Adopt a rule of making each picture better than the last.

Taken from high viewpoint; snapped from a lifeguard's stand. Sun in front gave shadows that help composition. Verichrome negative.

COMPOSITION
WHAT IS IT?

Volumes have been written on the subject but it is felt that the average camera fan would like it all boiled down to a few paragraphs of highly practical, definitely helpful information.

Generally speaking, the "composition" of a picture is simply its arrangement. Some arrangements are made by purposely placing figures or objects. Others are made by choosing a point of view. You may move a camera a few inches or a few feet and change the composition decidedly. Again, composition may be affected at the moment when the picture is made; when objects are moving the instant of "taking" controls the arrangement.

In the case of an outdoor scene, time of day will affect composition, for light and shadow become part of the arrangement. A good composition at eleven in the morning may be a poor composition at three in the afternoon, for shadows have a form, and light has an emphasis. They lead the eye to the point of special interest. They must not do this, however, the way the spokes of a wheel lead you to the hub. The eye must not suspect *how* it is being led. But it should like being led.

Outlines are important and to make clear what is meant by outlines we have taken a few pictures and diagrammed their principal lines—those that are most conspicuous to the eye (see page 64).

If a picture can be diagrammed in this way and the diagram, by itself, is agreeable as to balance, the composition is likely to be good.

Balance does not mean *sameness*. The lines may be full of "accident" and change, but the general balance, when it is right, gives a satisfaction such as we feel in the irregularity of a tree.

It is to be remembered also that the outer edge of a picture is part of its composition. The "holes" or open spaces inside the margin should have variety of shape. Lines should disappear into the margin at agreeably varied points. When they do this best the diagram may be turned upside down and still seem pleasing in itself. Thus a good composition may be guessed at long range before you know what the picture is about.

Can good composition come by accident? Sometimes. It may happen because all of our ideas of beauty come from the natural.

63

A viewpoint to include only section outlined in white would have been better.

The dotted outlines indicate how lines of subjects converge finally to center of action or interest: girl's face, chicks feeding, toy trains, and bubble.

After all, in pictorial composition there are but a few basic principles that, if remembered, will aid anyone to make attractive pictures.

Have but one main or dominating point of interest. Do not try to make a picture tell more than one story. The principal subject may be one person or several, a nearby pond or a distant mountain; but whatever it is, give that subject proper prominence and have all else that may be included in the picture area subordinated or given a position of minor importance.

There should be objects of secondary interest in a picture unless it is a close-up portrait or a straight record. For instance, if the picture is of a group of trees, a second group, or other objects, a little farther away

Study, also, the three pictures at the right; each has good composition. Point of view and lighting are important elements.

will help toward balance. When people are in the picture and the principal thing you wish to photograph is a waterfall, for example, they should not look at the camera but at the waterfall and they should not be nearer to the camera than approximately twenty-five feet.

LOOK BEYOND THE SUBJECT— YOUR CAMERA LENS WILL

The background for a figure or group may be a clump of bushes, a pretty landscape, a shoreline, or a doorway, but it must not attract as much attention as the principal subject. On the contrary, it should merely be a setting or frame for it. Peculiar and distracting effects are sometimes obtained if you disregard what is beyond or back of the subject. Be sure, for example, that from the position of the camera lens a tree branch does not seem to be growing out of the head of the person whose picture you are taking. Again, beware of an uncovered trellis or arbor when taking little informal portraits or storytelling groups. Prominent horizontal or vertical lines always detract. The clapboarded side of a house also is not so good when taking reasonably close up pictures of people. Garden bushes and other foliage make better backgrounds.

TONES ARE IMPORTANT

A good picture should also be well balanced in the matter of light and shade. Gradations of tones from light to dark are needed, and portions of each should be distributed in the picture so that it will appear well balanced. For example, all of the dark tones should not be in one place.

65

A wide range of well-balanced tones, unusualness of design, yet simplicity of subject, made this especially interesting.

A reasonable equalization of light and dark tones is needed.

Bear in mind that there should not be two bright spots or dark spots of the same importance in a picture and that the dominant part of the picture area is just a trifle away from the center. The horizon line in a landscape should never divide a picture into two equal parts. It is best to have it one-third from the top or bottom. Experience and searching criticism of pictures, as you progress, will teach much. Just bear in mind that composition is, in the final analysis, simply the selection and arrangement of objects within the picture area.

Is the picture pleasing to look at? That is, are the objects in such positions, in relation one to another, as to make an agreeable effect? Can you tell at a glance what the picture portrays?

If you can say "yes" to these questions, it is safe to assume that the picture has reasonably good composition.

All lines lead to center of interest.

THAT THIRD DIMENSION EFFECT

AN AID TO INTERESTING COMPOSITION

W<small>HEN</small> making a picture, it is not necessary to forever abide by the advice to have the light come from over the shoulder. While this is good for the beginner, you can gradually depart from the rule. Those of us who like to try breaking such rules have found that most of the work of which we are proud has been produced under other lightings. The important thing to remember is that you must never stand so that sunlight will strike into the lens.

The lighting of the subject has much to do with securing that quality sometimes called "atmosphere" in a picture. There are a number of ways in which a photograph may be given apparent depth or third dimension. Taking the picture when there are long shadows, getting a reflection in the foreground, using strong side-lighting or back-lighting, and timing the exposure just right so that the detail of objects in shadow is not blocked out are precautions that contribute to the desired effect. Let us consider each of these separately.

Shadows, thrown in long drawn-out splotches across walls and walks,

67

more than anything else make one feel that he is "looking into" a picture instead of "looking on" a flat piece of paper carrying the images of the objects recorded. The foreground should be well broken up with shadows so that there is not too much contrast between it and the rest of the picture.

The Kodak Adjustable Lens Hood guards against flare in back-lighted pictures.

When a body of water can be included as a part of the foreground, then there are wonderful opportunities for adding depth. The reflection will carry one's attention back and away from the foreground—into the picture—and lead to the principal point of composition. Reflections often serve as an avenue to lead back from the foreground of a setting. The only precaution necessary when dealing with a water foreground in strong sunlight is to watch that a swell or wave does not throw reflected light sparkles upon the lens, as that may fog the picture.

Side-lighting, where the source of illumination comes from the side of the object or scene, and back-lighting, where the light comes from the rear, are not difficult to handle if the lens is protected from the light coming toward it. Shade the lens with the hand, stand in the protecting shadow of a tree or better still use a Kodak Lens Hood

when making such exposures. Also, you should time the exposure more for the parts in shadow than for those that are highlighted.

Along the roads and trails of forest where long spears of sunlight pierce into the shadows, good opportunities for striking pictures possessing depth are plentiful. Note the picture at the top of page 82.

Heavy shadows contribute much to third dimension quality.

68

FOR PICTURES THAT ARE DIFFERENT

THE UNUSUAL VIEWPOINT

VIEWPOINT means much and is an important factor in picture making. It has much to do with the perspective we get in pictures. If the perspective is not pleasing to the eye, it will not be pleasing in the picture, and if the effect as seen from the viewpoint of the camera lens is odd or startling it will be recorded just so in the picture.

69

Winding staircases and winding roads present material for pictures that are different. Without the figures these would not have been so interesting.
AT BOTTOM: *Note how all lines lead to the point of interest.*

While bad drawing and distortion are to be avoided in the truly artistic photograph, it is possible to obtain many interesting pictures from unusual points of view even though the perspective be a bit violent. Expert photographers are today finding new angles from which to make their pictures, and for the most part the results are pleasing as well as attractive and unusual. Many amateurs are also finding a new interest in picture making from this effort to get something different. They, too, are "shooting" from positions that are daring and new.

Notice the illustrations in newspapers and magazines by leading advertisers. Bold, odd, forceful, fantastic, and withal, different!

This radical departure probably started with the professional motion picture camera operator who ignored all previous so-called "iron bound" rules of the game. The first thing he did was to "shoot" *into* the light. Next, he made pictures from odd angles, obtaining "worm's-eye" as well as "bird's-eye" views.

Light filters and "Pan" film helped him to get striking and artistic effects in his pastoral and travel scenes. The pictorial photographer followed, cautiously, but surely; and in today's salons of pictures made by photography we are treated to a variety of new and, for the most part, decidedly pleasing material, most of which is the work of small, collapsible, hand type cameras.

Now the amateur snapshooter is doing things he never thought of undertaking before. He finds that by shading his lens from the glare of the sun he, too, can make charming back-lighted pictorial records. For many subjects he has disregarded the rule to hold the camera level— he points it up or down at severe angles—and though in some instances he may get weird effects from untrue horizontal or vertical lines, the results are nevertheless interesting; mainly perhaps because they are startling and different, though actually some may be more natural than if made in the ordinary way.

This sort of thing is not, however, recommended for the beginner. It is better first to acquire an understanding of the fundamentals by using the camera as advised in the instruction booklet. After that he may experiment with odd angles and unusual lighting effects and will soon obtain many out-of-the-ordinary pictures.

Head on, for this subject, would not have been nearly as effective as this oblique view. **71**

Winter Haze.

STREET
PHOTOGRAPHY
and Architectural Studies

THE successful picturing of street scenes and of story-telling incidents about the city is another interesting phase of outdoor picture making for the amateur. He must bear in mind that he will have to work quickly and quietly, attracting as little attention as possible where people are to be included, and he must be able to take in an interesting

72

situation at a glance. The picture below, left, is a very good example.

The ability to level the camera quickly and accurately is particularly important, as in most instances the architecture of the surrounding buildings will show, and if the camera is not level, the building lines will be anything but pleasing.

A good many pictures of street scenes show that a number of persons were looking at the camera when the exposure was made. For instance, take a group of youngsters interested in some game; their action, intensity and unconsciousness are what make the picture. Let them become aware of your purpose, the game stops and all stare at the camera, thus spoiling the opportunity for a successful bit of work.

The position of the camera is also important. Many pictures of street scenes show that the point of view from which they were taken was too low. Often a good shot of a busy street can be made from the steps of some public building. Interesting and odd views are obtained from the windows of high buildings, pointing the camera down.

When taking streets from the curb, hold the camera as high as you can. Cameras with eye-level finders are especially convenient for this kind of work. Don't take the picture when a fast-moving vehicle is very near.

General views of streets in business sections of a city or of streets in a residential section are easy to make and add variety to one's collection. Care should be taken in the former to use a shutter speed sufficient to arrest the action and in the latter to guard against underexposure, because of the cutting off of light by tree foliage, as in the pictures on page 57.

Repairmen, sidewalk scenes, and skylines add variety to the picture record of your town. A Kodak Lens Hood can be used to advantage when the sun is in front of camera.

ARCHITECTURAL STUDIES

Camera owners, particularly tourists, frequently encounter architectural subjects possessing interesting features from the structural and historic points of view. Then, too, there probably are attractive buildings right in your own town or city which would make good picture material; the churches, city hall or court house, the new bank or office buildings, and, of course, your own home.

In most architectural work full detail is essential, in which case the lens should be stopped down to the smallest opening consistent with light conditions and the 1/25 second shutter speed used.

This branch of picture taking requires that the camera be held level if vertical lines are to be kept straight and the building pictured in correct drawing and perspective. What happens when the camera is tipped up is shown on page 36. The picture below, left, is definitely an "angle" shot.

Often the foliage of trees on the grounds forms a pleasing vista through which the edifice may be framed. An attractive building should be pictured from several angles.

The early morning and late afternoon hours of a sunny day are especially favorable for picturing architectural subjects as it is during these hours that long shadows add much to pictorial effect.

While you will want at least one view of the entire building from a good vantage point, it is not always necessary to include the whole of the structure in your picture to portray some interesting bit of architectural detail, such as a doorway section alone.

The Kodak Pictorial Diffusion Disk (see below, right, and page 82) can be used to advantage in architectural work to pleasingly soften the focus and add artistic value.

74

An angle shot of a skyscraper in the making, the avenue from atop a bus and a diffused architectural study.

LANDSCAPES

Hᴇʀᴇ, as in all photographic work, indiscriminate "snapshooting" is not conducive to either good work or the early acquisition of practical knowledge. First there should be a reason for taking the picture; either to preserve a record of some interesting place or occasion, to portray some attractive bit of scenic beauty, or to produce a picture appealing to the observer by its charm of line and tone. While a picture may combine all these qualities only one of them should be dominant and there should never be any question as to why the picture was made.

There are several points in regard to artistic composition that the beginner must keep in mind if he is to secure results that are satisfactory pictorially as well as technically. Good composition, so important in landscapes, is, as mentioned heretofore, simply the bringing together of things in an orderly and symmetrical arrangement and its general principles can be applied in such a way that they will aid materially in avoiding the inartistic in scenics.

TWO PICTURES IN ONE

One of the faults most often seen in the work of the beginner is the desire to include too much within the confines of the picture. There is frequently material for two or even more complete pictures crowded into one, with the result that the eye wanders confusedly from one point to another, producing a sense of irritation rather than pleasure. See page 63.

Selection, the leaving out of what is really not required, is the first lesson, then, to be learned. The viewpoint should be chosen carefully, remembering that much that is extraneous may be eliminated or at least made unobtrusive by moving the camera to the right or left, up or down, nearer or farther away, by focusing for different

The horseman, in the top picture, adds life-interest and aids composition.

The fence shadows in the winter road scene help to lead the eye into the picture and "break up" what might otherwise be too much white space in the foreground.

76

planes; and by using a different diaphragm opening in the lens.

Simplicity may well be considered the basis of artistic work. Over-crowding should be avoided and as few lines and masses as possible included within the picture area. Ordinarily a picture should have but one dominant object, group, or mass of principal interest, all others being subordinated but helping to support it. However, when a snapshot must of necessity include more than is required for good composition, it can be improved immensely by a judicious masking of the negative, especially when making an enlargement.

DON'T DIVIDE PICTURE IN HALF

Strive, however, for such a combining of the masses, tones, and lines to produce a pleasing general effect. Objects should be so grouped that there will not be two shadows or highlights of equal importance. As a general rule, neither a horizontal nor a vertical line should ever exactly divide the picture space into two equal parts. When there are subjects in the near foreground the horizon line might well be about one-third from the top as this gives prominence to the foreground.

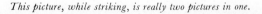

There are usually exceptions to rules. In the picture below the large expanse of clouded sky is balanced by but a small section of foreground but the dark tones are dramatic, forceful. Note also that this picture could be divided in half, vertically.

A roadway or stream should preferably be taken from an angle and include a curve if possible, since curved lines are more beautiful than straight ones. It should not divide the picture into two equal parts, but, if entering near a lower corner, will lead the eye into the picture and so be helpful to the composition (see pages 70, 76).

77

This picture, while striking, is really two pictures in one.

From a Pan Film negative with K1 Filter on lens; 1/25 second, stop 11.

The picture should balance both vertically and horizontally, a large mass near the center being balanced by several smaller objects on the other side or by a single smaller one farther from the center. The exact center is always the weakest spot, the most important position for the principal object being a little to one side or in some cases slightly above or below the center.

Clouds are always a decided pictorial asset inasmuch as they break up the monotony of a white sky and add greatly to the beauty and attractiveness of the picture. When it is desired to emphasize the clouds a sky filter or color filter should be used over the lens. Details about the uses and advantages of filters in landscape work are given on pages 84 to 95.

LIGHTING

Lighting is of equal importance with the arrangement of the objects in the picture. It is the variation in the lights and shadows that gives the picture depth and roundness, making the subject stand out from its surroundings. Usually the shadows should be transparent, to a degree, but full of detail. This is obtained by a rather full exposure.

A beginner when making exposures in the sunlight should have the sun a little to one side behind him. If the illumination comes from directly back of the camera, the shadows are more or less lost, giving a flat appearance. When you are a little more advanced, try some early morning or late afternoon shots. These times of day present opportunities for splendid pictorial studies because of the slanting shadows, as mentioned before. Especially attractive shots may be made from a position where the shadows fall toward your camera rather than away from it. In "back-lighted" work of this kind, be sure that no sun rays strike into the camera lens. The Kodak Lens Hood, previously mentioned, is of distinct advantage in making these pictures.

In such work give a bit more exposure than would be needed if the sun were directly on the front of the subject. Perhaps the next larger sized stop opening will let in enough more light to record the detail desired in the shaded parts, or, if using a small stop for a gain in depth of focus, a slow automatic exposure, 1/10, or a very short time exposure will yield an excellent negative. "SS" Pan Film has an advantage at these times of day in addition to its complete color sensitiveness in that it is about 50% faster than ordinary film in the soft yellow light, and shorter exposures may therefore be used.

FIGURES IN SCENICS

Some workers believe that landscape pictures are made more interesting when figures that are not a natural part of the landscape are included.

Others believe that when the scenic is right in composition and properly balanced in tones nothing else is required. Whether to include a figure, then, depends entirely upon your personal liking.

Vistas are always appealing. Detail in the tree trunks was not desired here. 1/25 second at f.22, brilliant light. Verichrome Film.

The figures in each of these pictures add interest and in the one above are the definite story point of the subject.

There may be times when something is needed in the foreground or middle distance for balancing the composition or for emphasizing the point of interest.

In still other types of landscape and marine pictures it is a debatable question as to whether the introduction of a figure would enhance them at all. The pictures on pages 78 and 79 are such subjects.

The writer has opportunity to see hundreds of pictures of the kind we have been discussing and in his opinion an improvement would be had in many if a figure had been located somewhere in the foreground.

THIS "HUMAN INTEREST" ELEMENT

Take a good look at the picture on the next page (at left). Now place the tip of your finger over the image of the man. Quite a change, isn't it? Something happens; the scene becomes a bit desolate though all the beauty of nature is still there. How about lost companionship? Is that a part of it? Perhaps, but not all. As you looked at the picture were you not, in the subconscious mind, standing and drinking in with him the grandeur of the mountain? Our companion vanishes and we probably sense a sort of loneliness. That is not all, however, in this particular picture, for the light-toned figure of the man or some other object was needed in the dark foreground to give balance. Had the

80

stream of water, beside which he is standing, photographed in a light tone, an additional object at this point might not have been required. Composition would probably have been even better in this setting if the man had been over to the left more—well beyond the center and perhaps a little nearer the lower edge of the picture. The inclusion of an object of known size will also readily give a true relationship of sizes of other objects in the picture.

How about the old-world street scene? Would not a figure, say, of an old woman trudging along with a bundle of fagots over her shoulder add interest and story-telling value? A space has been marked on the print to indicate where the figure might have been.

Of course, to have any subject you use as an incidental figure in such a picture too near or looking at the camera is a mistake. The picture would then become two things: a portrait and a scenic, and the interest would be so much divided that the picture would hardly be acceptable from either angle.

Animals such as horses, cows, sheep, or deer can frequently be included successfully in scenics.

Does the figure help the picture?

Would a figure at X help this?

When one is alone on a picture-seeking excursion, he may wish that he could place a figure at a certain spot for balancing; or for lending a point of interest to the composition. By letting a Kodak Self Timer make the exposure, the photographer can place himself on that spot and thus secure his picture, composed just as he wants it.

ARTISTICALLY DIFFUSED LANDSCAPE PICTURES

Pictures with pleasingly softened lines, yet retaining all the needed detail, can be made with any camera by merely placing a supplementary lens over the regular camera lens.

Most Kodak enthusiasts prefer moderation in the diffusing of images of subjects that are suitable for such treatment.

There is a vast difference between a properly diffused picture and what might be termed a "fuzzygraph." With the proper kind of diffusion, detail will not be obliterated but will merely be artistically softened. Yet the entire picture image will gain in roundness and depth and take on more of the aforementioned stereoscopic effect.

When the shadows in a strongly lighted view are made more luminous, the critically sharp edges broadened, and the tones more gradually blended, the picture takes on life and realness. It has just a bit more of that elusive third-dimension quality we have discussed on page 67.

A simple way to obtain proper diffusion, in scenics, with the characteristics mentioned, is by the use of the Kodak Pictorial Diffusion Disk. No change whatever is required in focusing nor does the disk necessitate the lengthening of exposure.

The grooved lines on the glass of the disk do not extend all the way to the center, so that there is a small area that is perfectly plain. No diffusion will result if the camera lens should be stopped down so far that the rays of light that are reflected from the subject to the lens pass through this central area only. On the other hand, when the camera lens is used wide open (at its largest stop) the utmost diffusion of which the lens is capable will be obtained.

Binding a Filter and a Diffusion Disk together.

Thus the photographer can readily introduce much or little diffusion into his pictures, as the amount secured depends upon the stop.

The lighting of a scene has much to do with the effectiveness of soft focus pictures. Results are likely to be disappointing if such pictures are made on a dull, cloudy day. Then there are no shadows or contrasting highlights, and the pictures will be lifeless.

The Kodak Pictorial Diffusion Disk has a tendency to soften harsh lightings. Any brightly lighted, nearby landscape will be an especially good subject as the contrast between highlights and shadows will be reduced, and the tonal values recorded more as the eye sees them.

DIFFUSION AND COLOR CORRECTION

Clouds also seem to appear more real when the disk is employed. To obtain color correction in addition to diffusion, the disk may be used in combination with a color filter by binding the two together, face to face, with adhesive tape. The Diffusion Disk side of this combination should be placed next to the camera lens. Enlargements from negatives of diffused and filtered subjects are especially suitable for coloring.

83

Filtered and Diffused.

COLOR FILTERS
THEIR SELECTION AND USE

From a Pan Film negative, K2 Filter used, 1/25 second, stop f.22.

WHEN a beam of white light, such as sunlight, is passed through a prism, it is split up into a band having the colors of the rainbow. These colors appear in the order of violet, blue, green, yellow, orange, and red. These are the visible colors; there are other rays that are not visible to the eye—the ultra-violet and the infra-red rays.

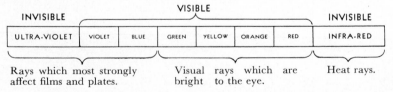

INVISIBLE			VISIBLE				INVISIBLE
ULTRA-VIOLET	VIOLET	BLUE	GREEN	YELLOW	ORANGE	RED	INFRA-RED

Rays which most strongly affect films and plates.　　Visual rays which are bright to the eye.　　Heat rays.

It is because of the varying effects these light rays have upon our eyes and upon photographic films that color filters are helpful and necessary to our photographic picture making. They do not, however, result in getting pictures in natural colors.

84

For general photography the infra-red rays can be disregarded (except for cutting out haze in long distance photography and for odd effects) because ordinary and even panchromatic films are not affected by them. On the other hand the ultra-violet rays have a very marked effect upon all films.

COLOR SENSITIVENESS OF FILMS

Kodak Regular N.C. Film is affected by those rays of the spectrum from the ultra-violet to the middle of the green. Kodak Verichrome Film responds similarly, although it is much more sensitive to the green rays and is also affected by yellow rays. Kodak Super Sensitive Panchromatic, Super X Panchromatic, and Panatomic Films respond to the ultra-violet and the whole of the visible spectrum, right through the red.

Even though the newer films have been made more sensitive in the green, yellow and red regions of the spectrum, they all have their greatest sensitivity in the blue, violet and ultra-violet regions. In this respect the sensitivity of photographic materials differs from that of the human eye.

AS SEEN BY THE EYE

The eye has its greatest sensitivity in the green, is less sensitive to blue and violet, and is not at all sensitive to ultra-violet. This accounts for the fact that an average landscape photographs differently with respect to tone values than the eye sees it. In a photograph of a landscape scene made on an ordinary film the trees appear abnormally dark, and the sky abnormally light. This is because light

from the sky is especially rich in blue, violet and ultra-violet to which the film is particularly sensitive, and to which the eye is comparatively insensitive. On the other hand, trees reflect much green light, to which the eye is very sensitive and to which the film is quite insensitive. The primary purpose of a color filter in landscape photography is to correct this state of affairs, and it is accomplished by using a filter which reduces the amount of ultra-violet, violet and blue light without reducing the amount of green light. The final result is a picture in which the tone values are almost the same as the eye sees them in the original subject.

WHAT THE FILTER DOES

The action of a filter is primarily the selective absorption of light of different colors. That is, rays of certain colors are allowed to pass through freely, while others are partially or wholly absorbed. This is the fundamental concept of a filter, and should be kept in mind whenever an occasion for using one arises. There are many different kinds of filters for many different purposes, but we shall deal here only with those which are most commonly used in landscape and pictorial work.

Because a filter selectively absorbs certain rays, it necessarily appears colored. A red book appears red, not primarily because it reflects red light, but because it *absorbs* light of other colors. A red filter appears red because it absorbs green and blue light. A filter which absorbs blue and red is green; one which absorbs only blue appears yellow because it transmits green and red light, and these affect the eye as yel-

Made on Verichrome Film, Kodak Sky Filter used over camera lens.

86

low. Since the most useful photographic filter reduces the amount of light in the blue region of the spectrum without appreciably reducing light of other colors, it appears yellow. However, all yellow transparent substances are not suitable as filters, because some may transmit freely the ultra-violet and yet appear identical with others which absorb it completely. It will be readily seen that the former are valueless as filters for this purpose.

MUST BE ACCURATELY MADE

Nearly all filters are made of a thin sheet of dyed gelatin cemented between two glasses. The reason for using dyed gelatin instead of colored glass is that a much wider and more useful range of filters can be made with the dyes that are available than can be made with the relatively limited number of colored glasses available. The dye which is used to make a filter is chosen, not from the color it appears to be, but after careful measurement of its spectral absorption characteristics. The sheet of gelatin filter is made with the utmost care, exactly the right amount of dye is used for a given amount of gelatin, and the finished sheet must have exactly the right thickness. The finished filter film is carefully inspected, and must come up to high standards of uniformity, clearness and freedom from minute imperfec-

tions. The dyed gelatin alone can be used, but it is so delicate that it must be handled with great care when being cut to be placed between lens elements. For this reason the filter mounted between glass is recommended for general use. Ordinary glass is not of sufficiently high quality to be used for this purpose, since the finished filter

Made on Pan Film, X1 Filter used over camera lens.

Relative color brightnesses as received by the eye. Upper left, red; upper right, yellow; immediately above the yellow, a green leaf; lower left, white; lower right, blue. Panchromatic Film, K2 Filter.

must be of optical quality comparable with the finest lens. The finished filter is thus seen to be not a mere bit of colored glass, but an accurately made optical unit.

KINDS OF FILTERS AND WHAT THEY DO

The filters recommended for use with Kodak Film are the K1, K2, the X1, X2, the N1, N2, N3, and N4, the Kodak Color Filter, the Kodak Sky Filter, the G and the A Filters. There are other filters but they are for more or less technical and specific purposes, and need not be mentioned here; they are described fully in the book, "The Photography of Colored Objects."

The K1 Filter is a pale yellow filter and is used as a correcting filter, when short exposure is of more importance than a high degree of correction.

The K2 Filter is a medium yellow filter giving a greater correction than the K1 and will bring out clouds more definitely. When used with Kodak Super Sensitive Panchromatic Film under daylight conditions, a very close approximation to the true orthochromatic rendering of the subject is obtained. It may also be used with Super X Panchromatic and Panatomic Films, although for the closest approximation to orthochromatic rendering another filter is more desirable as mentioned farther on. One of the merits of the K2 Filter is that it requires an increase in exposure of only two times when used with the panchromatic films.

THE KODAK COLOR FILTER is well adapted to average work, is useful in the elimination of haze and of particular advantage when brilliant cloud effects are desired. It gives more correction than the K1, and when used with Kodak Verichrome Film requires less increase of exposure than the K2 but gives about the same amount of correction. It is also well suited for use with panchromatic films. For the photographer who confines himself to one filter this is the one which should be obtained. The results in landscape photography are comparable with those obtained with the K2 Filter.

THE X1 FILTER is used on the few occasions when complete color correction in monochrome is required with Super X Panchromatic, and Panatomic Film with daylight. Such occasions arise when photographing bright yellows and reds when green is also present, as exemplified by flowers of these colors. Also, in making a close-up of a face against the sky, the X1 Filter is desirable. The use of a yellow filter in such cases may result in a chalky rendering of the flowers or face. The X1 Filter is useful when complete correction is desired, using Kodak Super Sensitive Panchromatic Film with artificial light. The X1 is a pale green filter and should not be used with Kodak Regular N.C. or Verichrome Film.

THE X2 FILTER has the same characteristics as the X1 Filter but to a more marked degree. It is used with Kodak Super X Panchromatic and Kodak Panatomic Films for correct color rendering in black-and-white with artificial light. It is not intended for use with daylight. Factors for this filter will be found in the instructions accompanying it.

THE G FILTER is a deep yellow "contrast" filter. It cuts through atmospheric haze still further than the K2 or the Kodak Color Filter and is of great advantage when there is considerable haze in distant landscape subjects. It is also useful in giving more contrast between

Panatomic Film negative, G Filter,
1/2 second, stop f.22.

snow and shadows in snow scenes, especially in weak sunlight.

THE A FILTER is a red filter and may be used to advantage for recording cloud forms against a blue sky. The results obtained with this filter when using Kodak Super Sensitive Panchromatic, Super X Panchromatic, and Panatomic Films show a greatly exaggerated contrast, but if the form of the clouds is all that is required, such an exaggeration is to be desired. It is not advisable to use so deep a filter generally in pictorial work.

THE KODAK SKY FILTER may be used to assist in recording clouds in landscape pictures without increasing the exposure. Only the upper portion is colored yellow and, therefore, the filter will tend to hold back the excess ultraviolet, violet, and some of the blue rays from the sky portion of the subject without appreciably affecting the light reflected from the foreground. This results in the blue sky photographing somewhat darker than without a filter and the white clouds consequently should stand out against it in better contrast. If, however, the exposure is excessive, the clouds may be lost even when using the filter. The Kodak Sky Filter, when turned with the yellow half at the bottom, is also helpful in getting contrast between sunlight and shadow in snow scenes.

This pale yellow Kodak Sky Filter is more effective with Kodak Regular N.C. and Verichrome Films than with panchromatic films. The effect is greatest with small stop openings. The Kodak Sky Filter is not intended to be used as a general purpose filter.

THE N1, N2, N3, and N4, FILTERS are for the Kodak Retina.

N1 and N2 are light yellow and medium yellow respectively. N3 is green and N4 is orange. They are for use with panchromatic films. The N4 is only for haze cutting in distant landscapes.

FILTER FACTORS

Since a filter absorbs some of the light which would otherwise reach the film, the exposure must be increased. The "filter factor" is a measure of the amount of light absorbed by a filter with respect to the amount transmitted. The filter factor represents the number of times the exposure must be increased when using a filter as compared with the exposure required without it. A filter having a factor of 2 with, say, Kodak Panatomic Film, will thus require twice the exposure necessary without it.

The filter alone does not determine the factor. It is necessary to take into consideration the color sensitivity of the film which is to be used. For example, the filter factor of the G Filter for panchromatic films in daylight is only $2\frac{1}{2}$; for Verichrome Film, it is about 5; for Kodak Film (Regular) it is 24, which is beyond the practicable range of usefulness. Below is given a table of daylight filter factors of the commonly used filters with the different Kodak Films.

FILTER FACTORS FOR DAYLIGHT			
Filter	Kodak Film (Regular)	Kodak Verichrome	Kodak "SS" Pan, Super X Pan, and Panatomic
K1	3	2	$1\frac{1}{2}$
Kodak Color Filter	4	2	$1\frac{1}{2}$
K2	5	$2\frac{1}{2}$	2
G	24	5	$2\frac{1}{2}$
A	—	—	4
X1	—	—	5
*N1	—	—	$1\frac{1}{2}$
*N2	—	—	2
*N3	—	—	$2\frac{1}{2}$
*N4	—	—	3

*For Kodak Retina only.

A Kodak Bantam Special shot from a plane of a plane.
1/500 second at f.6.3, Panatomic Film, K1 Filter.

DISTANT LANDSCAPES

In landscape work, the yellow filter, as mentioned heretofore, performs a valuable function. It gives sharper, clearer detail in distant objects. On the majority of summer days, the distant hills and other objects in a landscape appear somewhat hazy. If they are photographed on ordinary films without a filter, they appear "flat," without detail, and seem to blend together. This is because the haze scatters blue light and so tends to blur the detail of objects seen through it, that it appears as if they were viewed through a fine ground-glass window.

It so happens that, while haze scatters blue light, it scatters green light very little, and red light still less. So, if we use a yellow filter over our lens to cut down the blue light, and take the picture by green, or green and red light, we shall be able to photograph through the haze, and the detail in the distant objects will be sharper.

This is done to a marked degree by using the K2 or the Kodak Color Filter with Kodak (Regular) and Verichrome Films. A decided improvement in detail results. Panatomic and "SS" Panchromatic and Super X Pan Films are very sensitive to green and red light. Even without a filter they are able to "see" through the haze to some extent. With a yellow filter, however, especially the Kodak Color Filter or the K2, they reproduce the detail of objects very clearly.

It will also be seen from what has been said of the G Filter that it is particularly useful in photographing landscapes. It cuts through atmospheric haze still further than the other yellow filters and is of particular advantage when there is considerable haze in the distance.

From the foregoing it will be seen that the use of a yellow

"SS" Pan Film negative, K2 Filter, 1/25 second, stop f.8.

93

filter in landscape photography (1) reproduces clouds against the sky; (2) records the tones of colored objects (flowers, etc.) more nearly as the eye sees them; (3) gives better detail in distant objects.

RECORDING THE CLOUDS IN YOUR LANDSCAPE PICTURES

Landscape pictures are greatly enhanced by the inclusion of cloud formations. Present day negative materials record clouds to a certain extent even without the use of a color filter, but unless the clouds contain considerable gray or are heavily tinted with orange and red (as near sunset) a color filter will be needed to register them in their full beauty against a blue sky.

A typical cloud and sky recording, without a filter.

The same scene as taken with a K2 Filter over the lens.

The considerable contrast given by the Wratten A Filter.

Suppose we were photographing a landscape with billowy white clouds in the sky, and we used a film which responded only to ultra-violet, violet, and blue light. In our picture we should not be able to distinguish between the clouds and the sky if we gave enough exposure to record detail in the landscape. This is because the light from the blue sky and from the white clouds is very rich in the light rays which most strongly affect the film.

Although clouds and blue sky are both rich in ultra-violet, violet, and blue, there is a marked difference between the two. The light from clouds, being white, actually contains a lot of green and red light, while that from the blue sky does not. This, then, suggests a way of distinguishing between clouds and blue sky in a photograph. We must use a film which will respond to green, or to green and red light, and put over our lens a filter which does not let through the ultra-violet, violet, and blue. The green or green and red light from the clouds will

94

thus affect our film, while practically no light from the sky will get through to it, and in the print, the clouds will appear whiter than the sky.

Kodak Film (Regular) is somewhat sensitive to green light; Verichrome is more sensitive to the green, and Kodak "SS" Pan and Panatomic Films will respond to green to an even greater extent and also to red light. All these materials will, therefore, show up the clouds against the sky quite effectively if used with a yellow filter.

Only a light yellow filter, such as the Kodak Sky Filter or the K1 filter, will be needed to properly accentuate vivid and well defined cloud formations in a clear blue sky. The sky filter, which is described on page 90, is unique in that no increase in exposure time is needed and snapshots can be made with it with any camera. Both the K2 Filter and the Kodak Color Filter are especially useful in recording cloud forms that do not stand out vividly. Either of these makes a good general purpose filter.

The deeper the yellow color of the filter the more violet and blue it removes, or "holds back," and consequently the bigger the factor; that is, the more the exposure must be increased (see table page 91).

If night effects or decidedly dramatic sky tones are desired use the red A Filter, referred to on page 90. This filter and the G Filter may also be used for certain exaggerated sky effects in connection with the Kodak Pola-Screen referred to on page 96.

95

THE KODAK POLA-SCREEN

Kodak Pola-Screen, Type 1A,
Series V, with Lens Hood.

The purposes of the Kodak Pola-Screen, Type 1A, are to control sky brightness and to minimize oblique reflections.

Many natural things, photographed through the screen, assume a strange beauty, which may be observed through the screen while rotating it.

Our eyes respond naturally to differences in color and in intensity of light, and it is by these differences that we are able to see the world around us. There is another property in which light rays may differ, but our eyes, unaided, cannot see those differences. This property is called "polarization," and is concerned with the manner in which the light ray vibrates. It happens that clear skylight is partly polarized. Light rays may be polarized by optical devices; they are also partly polarized by reflections from common objects. Hence, much of the light by which we see things is polarized to some extent, a fact we first realize when we look through a Kodak Pola-Screen.

Besides having the power to polarize light, the Kodak Pola-Screens have the ability to control the intensity of light already polarized. A Pola-Screen over the lens, therefore, affords control of oblique reflections, and can also serve as a variable depth filter for dark sky effects.

96

WITHOUT POLA-SCREEN:
Oblique reflections obliterate detail
on side of house.

WITH POLA-SCREEN:
Oblique reflections subdued
and detail is recorded.

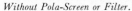

Without Pola-Screen or Filter.   *With Pola-Screen and an A Filter.*

USES IN AMATEUR PHOTOGRAPHY

Night effects may be secured by adding a red A Filter to the Pola-Screen. The G Filter is also useful. Intermediate settings, by revolving the screen, will give various depths of sky tones.

Other uses for the Pola-Screen by the amateur photographer are shown in the comparative pictures on these pages. The Kodak Pola-Screens, Type 1A, will also be found useful in photographing obliquely through glass or objects under water; for subduing oblique reflections which hide surface details, to show texture or pattern; and for architectural work. Faces, blossoms, trees and mountains can be made to stand out against darkened skies in a most dramatic manner.

With the Pola-Screen there is no distortion of color values of foreground objects. The only thing affected is sky depth. The direction of greatest effectiveness for the Pola-Screen in sky work is when the camera is pointing at right angles to the sun's rays. It is not effective when the camera is pointing toward the sun or directly away from it. The Pola-Screen has no more darkening effect on an overcast sky than does an ordinary color filter.

Many subjects photographed in full color, on Kodachrome Film, are made more striking when the sky is darkened by a Pola-Screen.

97

A SLIGHT EXPOSURE INCREASE

With a Pola-Screen in front of the lens, it is necessary to increase the exposure by using the next larger diaphragm opening than would be required without it. If two Pola-Screens are placed in front of the lens, with indicator handles parallel, it is necessary to use a diaphragm opening of one and a half times larger. This rule applies to all kinds of film. Full details and instructions accompany each Kodak Pola-Screen.

For the very advanced worker and commercial photographer, Pola-Screens are also available for use in front of the lights that illuminate subjects in laboratory or studio. For these photographers, special printed matter is available.

"DWARFED"

Aside from a splendid photograph pictorially the story told in the view opposite is at once grasped, in that humans are dwarfed beside nature's most picturesque representative—a tree.

The motif of the composition of the picture is repetition. The grandeur and height of the poplars are strikingly emphasized by the small figures. Notice the repetition in the relative heights of figures and trees.

Aside from the picture's subtle story value it is

excellent photographically, though it could have been spoiled by poor printing. The foreground was "dodged in" a bit for correct tone balance.

The sky and cloud recordings are of tone that likewise give good balance and afford a suitable and pleasing background.

Kodak "SS" Pan film was used with a K2 filter—1/25 second at f.11. A Diffusion Disc was used in making the enlargement from which this engraving was made.

98

PICTURING THE FLOWERS

IN THE HOME GARDEN AND AFIELD . . . .

Hazy light, 9.30 A. M., 1/5 second, stop f.22. Kodak "SS" Pan Film.

Successful flower photography is easy today for the amateur. With correct methods in picturing flowers the Kodak becomes a valuable assistance to the garden enthusiast and to the person who seeks out the wild flowers.

There are the records that can be made month by month of the rotation of bloom, the pictorial effect of certain plantings, the study of individual specimens for botanical research, the study of decorative design and pattern, and records of plantation for identification of varieties.

Then there are numbers of uses to which flower pictures may be put aside from record purposes and the adding of interest and variety to the pages of albums. Contact prints may be used for the making of artistic greeting or place cards for various occasions. Enlarged and tinted with Velox Water Colors or Kodak Transparent Oil Colors, flower pictures make attractive wall decorations for living room or den.

The introduction of Kodak "SS" Pan Film and Kodak Panatomic Film has made it possible for persons with limited experience and ordinary camera equipment to obtain strikingly beautiful results. The tone rendering qualities of these new films, even without the use of filters, have broadened the field of activities for those who wish to enjoy the fascination of flower photography. This does not mean that filters no longer have a use in this work, but it does mean that in many cases a filter is not needed. In others the use of a filter gives just enough more color correction to give the true rendition of tone values, in the black and white print, that are comparable to those seen by the eye. While these films, which are sensitive to all colors, are best for flower pictures, good results can also be obtained

Snow-in-Summer. Bright but no sun, 1/10 second, stop f.22 with Portrait Attachment; "SS" Pan Film.

with Verichrome Film and the proper filter, such as the Kodak Color Filter or the K2 Filter. See page 91 for filter factors.

USEFUL ACCESSORIES

Perhaps the most important accessory in picturing flowers, with the ordinary camera, is a Kodak Portrait Attachment, which permits working close up to the subject and thereby gives a much larger image in the picture than could ordinarily be obtained. Those who are expert prefer to use small diaphragm openings in order to give critical definition and depth of field, and time their exposures accordingly.

Magnolia, white with tinge of mauve. Late afternoon sunlight, 1/5 second, stop f.22, Kodak Portrait Attachment, "SS" Film.   101

For anything slower than 1/25 second the camera should, of course, be placed on a firm support. Some workers prefer a tripod, which can readily be adjusted to any height. Others find the handy Kodapod or Optipod quite satisfactory. Either of these may be used with equal success by merely attaching to a stick driven into the ground. Where a color filter is to be used in combination with a Portrait Attachment the two can be fastened together, face to face, with a piece of adhesive tape as shown in the illustration on page 83. When using this combination the Portrait Attachment side should, of course, be slipped over the camera lens.

LIGHTING

Proper lighting is the foundation for good flower photography. It should be remembered that shadows are necessary to properly reproduce form in any graphic illustration. In outdoor photography natural lighting is depended upon, and therefore, it is necessary that the light come from the right direction for the particular subject to be photographed. As a general rule, bright direct overhead light is not desirable, so the best results are obtained in the earlier morning hours or toward the end of the day when the direction of light is from the side. A hazy day, when the sun is under light clouds, is an ideal time for flower photography. As the blossoms usually turn towards the sun, the camera should be placed

TOP: *The Yucca Tree, taken from low position. Pan Film, K2 Filter.*
CENTER: *The Water Lily, taken from a boat. Pan Film.*
BELOW: *Poppies, taken with a gray card background, Verichrome Film.*

102

at a position to include the delicate shadows cast by parts of the blossoms, and surrounding foliage.

SELECT . . . ELIMINATE

Do not be confused by a profusion of flowers. Unless you especially wish to picture a large cluster, refrain from the almost irresistible tendency to include too much within the picture area. A simple cluster of blooms, maybe one or two, will make a much more artistic and pleasing picture than a large number. It is important to observe carefully which side of a group of flowers shows the most

At night. Photoflash furnished the light.

artistic arrangement and the best lighting effect. Often, especially where wild flowers grow, it will be found that there is obtrusive foliage or objects in foreground or background which spoil the composition and prevent selective photography. Such things in the foreground should be carefully removed or pulled out of the way and tied back with string so as to disturb natural conditions as little as possible.

Objects in the background may either be removed or hidden by an artificial background. This may consist of a smooth cloth of some

Tree Peony. Dark mauve to very light tones. Bright light, but no sun, 1/10 second, stop f.22, Portrait Attachment.

103

Prunus Mexicanus. A sheet of dark gray cardboard provided a good background. See page 125.

neutral tint, a cardboard or a window shade of tan or green. In any case the background material must be perfectly smooth, as any wrinkles or lines would show plainly in the picture. The trunk of a large tree makes a pleasing background for certain woodland flowers. A square of cardboard or a window shade may be used as an accessory to good advantage where flowers are to be photographed indoors. If it is convenient to select a window facing the north, it will be found that the light is best and more constant there.

THE ILLUSTRATIONS

Greater care must be exercised when photographing small light colored flowers than the larger ones. For example, study the picture, Snow-in-Summer blooms, on page 101. There is represented a mass of small snow white flowers, which in this photograph stand out individually because there is a delicate shadow recorded in each one. It should be noted that this picture was made on a hazy day. If this picture had been made in bright sunlight, the flowers would appear almost as one mass of white with very little individual form visible.

The picture of the Lemon Lilies was made early in the morning on a bright day with the light coming from the side. The flowers facing the sun have their front portions brilliantly lighted, while the rear portion is delicately shaded by the curved petals in front. In the picture of the Tree Peony (page 103), the blossom is very much larger than that

104

of the other blooms illustrated. While this photograph was made on a somewhat hazy day, the light was intense, as it was made later in the morning than the others. The shadows in this picture are more pronounced and add much to its attractiveness.

Lemon Lilies. Side lighting, Kodak Portrait Attachment, Panatomic Film.

When making the picture of the branch of Prunus Mexicanus, opposite page, photographed on the tree, a gray cardboard as background was held in position to make the blossoms stand out vividly and it gave good separation so that the structure and characteristics of the individual branch of blossoms could be studied.

THE POSITION OF THE CAMERA

Visualize the flower as you would see it in a vase or on exhibition. Under such conditions you do not look down upon the flowers, but rather view them from the side. There is a happy medium in regard to the location of the Kodak. If the flower is low-growing, stoop until the form is pleasing to the eye, then place the camera in the same position.

There is one very outstanding reward for those who become interested in photographing flowers, and that is an increased appreciation of form, color, and lighting as revealed in the camera studies.

Variety of colors. Dull, no sun, 1/2 second, stop f.32; "SS" Pan Film.

105

INDOOR PICTURES
By Daylight

CAMERA STUDIES OF THE FAMILY

IT IS NATURAL that the pictures which interest us most are those taken in and around the home. They become increasingly valuable as a source of enjoyment in the future, calling to mind many happy occasions and associations.

Informal little pictures of the various members of the family amid familiar home surroundings can easily be made in any room that has a window through which unobstructed light from the sky enters.

An excellent portrait lighting is obtained by drawing the shades of all but one of the windows, and placing the subject near the unshaded window as shown in the diagrams on the following page.

Photoflood Lamps are valuable as an auxiliary light indoors in the daytime.

When a subject in the position shown in the diagrams on this page looks squarely at the camera, the light will fully illuminate, with almost equal brightness, a part of the cheek on the side of the face away from the window.

This lighting effect can be seen by standing directly in front of the camera. Observe the shadow cast by the nose and if it extends downwards and sideways, the lighting will be satisfactory, and give the desired effect of roundness to the face. If the shadow extends sideways only, the light is coming too much from the side and too little from the top. Such a lighting will make the face look flat. To remedy this, cover the lower half of the window with a sheet or a piece of muslin, to cut off some of the side light and make the light come downward at an angle of approximately 45 degrees. If this is necessary, do not include window in the picture.

A reflector (a sheet or table-cloth will do) should be placed about two feet from the subject as shown in the diagrams, for reflecting light to the shadow side of the face. The reflector can be held or thrown over a screen or chair.

Made at 8 feet from subject, exposure 1 sec., f.8, Verichrome Film.

Made at 3 feet, using Portrait Attachment. Exposure and film same as above.

The staircase served as a splendid locale for this charming informal portrait. Here a Photoflood Lamp supplemented daylight to give good illumination, where wanted, and to shorten the exposure; 1/2 second, stop f.8.

The angle at which the reflector faces the subject is important. It should reflect light to the front as well as to the side of the face. If it reflects light to the side of the face only, the lighting will not be pleasing, for the ear on the shadow side will be more brightly illuminated than the depression between the top of the cheek and the nose. The angle at which the reflector should be placed when the light is coming wholly from the side is shown in the diagrams on page 107.

POSING

A good portrait should be a good likeness, and the less posing that is attempted, the better the likeness will be. As a rule it is better to "pose" the chair, if the person is to sit, rather than to urge him to assume any particular attitude or expression. In most cases the best portraits are made when people take their own characteristic positions.

The chair in which the subject is to sit should not be placed squarely facing the camera. The seated figure should usually face diagonally to the camera and if a full front view of the face is desired, the head should be turned so that the face is directly towards the lens. The head can be turned as suggested, without the slightest discomfort. This will avoid the square-shoulder effect which is often unpleasing. In most cases, one shoulder should be shown more prominently than the other.

The effect of this is seen in the pictures on page 107. The square-shoulder effect is shown on page 113, though it is not objectionable in this picture. While it is often pleasing in the case of full length portraits of children, it is not as satisfactory in head and shoulder portraits of grown-ups.

BACKGROUNDS

The most appropriate backgrounds for portraits in the home are often furnished by the walls or draperies, if they do not contain conspicuous designs.

If plain backgrounds are preferred (see pages 113 and 119), any color of cloth that shows no pattern may be used. It should be placed not 109

A No. 20 Photoflash furnished practically all the light for this picture made on "SS" Pan Film. Lens opening was f.11. The flash was made from a point about three feet to the left of the camera.

less than three feet behind the subject and should be free from wrinkles or creases which would show in the picture. It may be hung from the picture moulding or suspended in any other convenient way.

EXPOSURE

While good portraits can be made indoors on sunny days with exposures as short as 1/5 second, with an *f*.6.3 lens at full aperture, and Verichrome Film, with the subject not more than three feet from the window, it is always better to give a longer exposure when possible. On bright days exposures of one to three seconds are recommended with the slower double lenses at their largest stop openings. With single lenses the exposure should be from two to six seconds with the largest stop. The camera should be placed on a rigid table or tripod, or supported by an Optipod, for exposures longer than 1/25 second. If this is not done the pictures will probably be blurred from movement of the camera during the time the shutter is open.

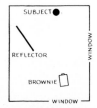

At Left Below: *Exposure 1/2 second, stop f.8; combination of daylight and artificial light. See diagram.*

At Right: *Exposure 3 seconds with Brownie camera. See diagram. Both on Verichrome Film.*

110

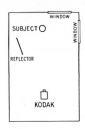

Subject 3 feet from sunlighted window, shade drawn down back of subject. See diagram. Use "SS" Pan Film, Kodak Anastigmat Lens at f.4.5 aperture. 1/25 second.

A CONVENIENT ACCESSORY

A very handy little accessory for indoor exposures is the Optipod pictured on page 51. It is felt-lined and clamps to any shelf, table, the back of a chair, or other support, and holds the camera firmly while the exposure is being made.

The ball-and-socket joint is a great convenience, since it permits tilting the camera to almost any angle.

It is possible, as shown in the illustration above, to make a snap-shot exposure (1/25 second) indoors, when light conditions are *unusually good*, with Kodaks fitted with an *f*.4.5 lens and loaded with "SS" Film.

If using a camera with a very fast lens like the *f*.2 or *f*.3.5 on the miniature Kodaks, snapshots can be made in many places around the house where there is exceptionally good light. By using the largest lens opening of these cameras, the subjects will not need to be so close to the window although it is advisable to use a reflector. With a little experience you will obtain surprisingly good pictures.

When using the 1/25 second on miniature Kodaks it is best to have the camera on a solid support. The Optipod, mentioned above, is very useful. Hand held you are likely to get slight image blur from camera movement.

111

KODAK PORTRAIT ATTACHMENT AND
KODAK DIFFUSION PORTRAIT ATTACHMENT

These attachments slip over the camera lens.

Both of these supplementary lenses enable you to make intimate close-ups; pictures within arm's length of the subject. Each gives a different rendition of the subject, but the way to use them is the same and the exposure required is the same as without the attachment.

The Kodak Portrait Attachment renders a *sharp image* close-up and makes possible head and shoulder portraits, such as those on the next page. It is also useful for photographing all sorts of small objects at short range, such as flowers, objects of art, and for making table-top studies.

The Kodak Diffusion Portrait Attachment yields very pleasing results in *soft focus*, as shown in the two lower pictures, next page, faithful to the subject in every detail, but with just enough diffusion of unpleasantly sharp lines and strong highlights to artistically soften and enrich the picture when such effects are desired. This attachment is not extreme in its action, and will not make unpleasant "fuzzy" pictures.

The attachments can be obtained from your Kodak dealer. Exact designation of camera, lens and shutter equipment is necessary when ordering by mail. Before using these attachments be sure to read the instructions that come with them.

TO PERMIT PICTURE TAKER TO GET INTO GROUP
AND FOR SELF-PORTRAITS

There are many occasions when the picture maker would like to be included in the photograph. This problem is easily solved with a Kodak Self Timer, referred to on page 50, a device that can be used with any camera fitted with a cable release. The picture at bottom of page 47 was made possible by the help of a Self Timer.

Attached to the cable release, the Kodak Self Timer can be so adjusted that it will "press the button" from half a second to one minute after it has been released. The Timer is only intended for making automatic exposures, that is, exposures that require but a single pressure

LEFT: *More light could have been reflected to side of child toward camera, but the picture is still very effective.*

BELOW: *Taken with the Kodak Diffusion Portrait Attachment. The pictures also show the effect of plain cloth as backgrounds, one light gray, one black.*

on the cable release for a given shutter adjustment.

For making indoor portraits with the Self Timer, without artificial light, it is best to use a camera which will make automatic exposures of half a second or one second, but as these timings are short for indoor portraiture, it will be necessary to use the largest stop opening and make the portraits on a bright day, with the subject close to a window which admits plenty of unobstructed light.

PORTRAIT STUDIES WITH WINDOW BACKGROUNDS

Probably few inexperienced amateurs would undertake to make indoor portraits with a window for a background and expect to obtain pictures that would show detail in the figure, detail in the furnishings beside the window and at the same time show the outdoor view seen through the window. Over the page are ways this can be done and the results are especially natural and pleasing.

113

Either a reflector or light from a Photoflood Lamp will illuminate the side of subject toward the camera if there are not windows nearby to aid.

Attractive indoor portraits, like that reproduced above, and those on pages 117 and 118 with a window as a background can be taken under light conditions that often exist in rooms that have windows on two sides.

The photographs can easily be made late in the afternoon when the atmosphere is hazy. The light from the western sky, while much stronger than the light from the south, is so softened by the haze that the contrast between sunlight and shadow outdoors is much less than it would be if the air were perfectly clear.

A reflector and artificial light are not required for aiding the illumination if there are nearby windows to counteract the light from the window in front of which your subject is placed and if light walls help to reflect light to the shadow side.

While a soft light is convenient for this kind of work it is not always necessary. Much depends upon the effect you desire; whether much or little detail is wanted in the side of the subject which is toward the camera.

The window-background pictures in this chapter show a variety of lightings. Some were made by sunlighted windows, others where the light was hazy and diffused by curtains. Much of course can be done to overcome decided contrasts by "dodging," or holding back, parts of such a negative when making the print or enlargement. Note the picture on page 118; this was a snapshot by a sunlighted window using "SS" Pan Film—1/25 second at stop *f*.4.5. Other windows in the room helped very little, but those and reflections from nearby walls gave enough balance and the fast film picked up sufficient detail. The snapshot exposure properly recorded the outdoor foliage.

Something to reflect light to the side of the subject toward the camera will be found an advantage when the window you are depending on for subject illumination is not near enough to give sufficient balancing light. A sheet thrown over a screen or highbacked chair and placed just out of the picture area will prove helpful.

THE PHOTOFLOOD OR PHOTOFLASH LAMP FOR AUXILIARY LIGHT

By using an abundance of artificial light in the room where you are making your window portrait studies, a very quick exposure can be given so that the outdoor scene, through the window, will not be overexposed and at the same time there will be sufficient illumination on the side of the subject which is toward the camera.

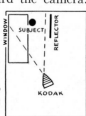

Exposure 1/5 *second, stop* *f*.4.5, *Kodak Verichrome Film negative. Note the diagram.*

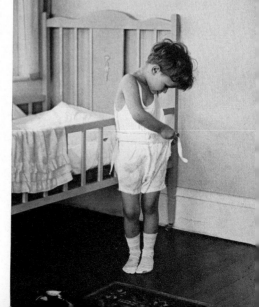

115

With plenty of light and a fast lens a snapshot exposure can easily be made.

The inexpensive Photoflood Lamps will be found very useful for this work in addition to their use for night pictures in the home, as referred to on pages 141 to 152. Then, too, you can use the Photoflash Lamp in making this kind of picture.

When using the Photo*flash*, it would be well to use one of the smaller openings in the lens so that during the interval of opening the shutter, flashing the lamp, and closing the shutter, the outdoor scene through the window will not record too heavily. The camera, of course, should be placed on a firm support and the subject should be cautioned not to move until the shutter is closed. If the subject does move, ever so slightly, the picture will be spoiled because of the registration of a secondary image.

GENERAL HINTS ON PORTRAITURE

The following paragraphs sum up the most important things to remember in making good informal studies of people indoors.

FULL EXPOSURE

In the somewhat contrasty light usually encountered it is better to err on the side of overexposure, as this not only affords better shadow detail, but the consequent tendency to "flatness" overcomes much of the contrast.

A GOOD LIKENESS

A portrait should be not only a correct likeness, but should present the subject in a pleasing pose, subduing defects and accentuating the strongest characteristics.

Pictures of people to be pleasing must avoid harsh contrasts and possess full gradation from highest light to deepest shadow; consequently you must so arrange your subject and light as to produce this effect.

STUDY THE LIGHTING

Placing your subject close to the window, with the light full on the face, you see that all parts are equally illuminated and consequently with no gradation. Now move the subject back a few feet; the light immediately softens, and you obtain a roundness and modeling far more pleasing.

116

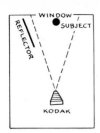

RIGHT: *See diagram above.* 1/25 *second, stop* f.8, *light from window diffused by curtains.*
BELOW: *Note diagram. Exposure* 1/25 *second, stop* f.4.5, *Verichrome Film.*

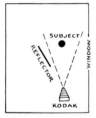

Turning the subject's head partly away from the light increases the steps in gradation; only the part of the face in deepest shadow appears too dark and without detail.

Illuminating this shadow is very simple. Take a large white towel and hold it about four feet away from the shadow side. It lightens the face a little, but not quite enough, so walk slowly toward the subject until this shadow is sufficiently illuminated to bridge that big gap in gradation.

All you have to do now is to pin this towel to the back of a tall chair or anything else handy.

Before attempting any exposures, place your subject in various parts of the room and study the effects you can produce.

LIGHT CONTROL

Always use the strongest light that you can that is consistent with the effect you desire to produce, as prolonged exposures not only detract from the spontaneity of expression and pose, but make your subject uncomfortable and liable to move.

In order that you may make your pictures *artistic*, you must learn how to control and direct the light just where you want it, to produce the desired effect.

It is generally accepted that allowing the light to fall on the face at an angle of forty-five degrees produces the most natural effect, and you can easily secure this illumination by simply blocking up the lower half of the window.

THE FACE IS THE THING

In portraiture you must always bear in mind that the face is the

1/25 *second, stop f.*4.5.
"SS" Pan Film.

118

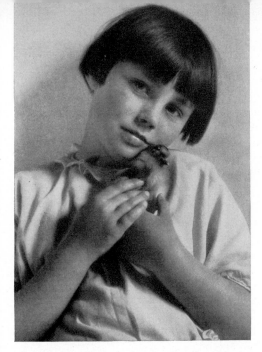

In this picture there is just enough softening of the lines, by the diffusion attachment, to enhance its attractiveness.

The Kodak Diffusion Portrait Attachment slips over the regular lens. Does not require any change in exposure.

most important element in the picture, and consequently you must subordinate all other parts. Sometimes an absolutely opaque curtain for the lower half of the window will suffice, but more often it will stop too much light, and in such cases, you may resort to the very simple expedient of using a piece of cheese cloth, or some other similar material, for curtaining off the lower portion of the window, employing one or more thicknesses, as the occasion demands.

CHILDREN (See also pages 42 to 50.)

Of course, in photographing small children, time exposures of any appreciable duration are out of the question, and in such cases, it is generally best to watch the subject keenly and at the slightest indication of movement close the shutter. The Kodaks with $f.6.3$, $f.4.5$, or faster lenses make it possible to get properly exposed negatives with relatively short exposures when the lens is used at its widest aperture, even snapshots at night, as discussed in a separate chapter.

Nine hundred and ninety-nine children out of every thousand are

naturally graceful and will pose themselves far better than you can—and right here remember two "dont's" —first, don't be in a hurry, and, second, don't be fussy. And patience—you must be Job plus.

The tactful photographer can coax his little subjects to the proper place for the exposure, and then wait until the right moment arrives.

When you were a youngster didn't you "just hate" to have any one fussing with or at you, pulling down your skirts or straightening your necktie or slicking back your hair or saying, "Don't do that, Jimmie," or "Take your finger out of your mouth, Susie"? Just remember your own childish likes and dislikes when picturing the youngsters and you'll get better pictures.

CLOTHING FOR CHILDREN

Simple costumes photograph best, and the children feel more natural in them. White and the lighter colors are especially well adapted for children's clothes. They add to the youthful appearance of the subject as well as help to cut exposure time to a minimum.

GROWN-UPS

When it comes to the grown-ups, a certain amount of posing may be necessary, though as you become accustomed to the work it may be minimized by so arranging the seat they are to occupy, or the other incidentals of your picture, that they will automatically assume the pose desired.

Full length and three-quarter length portraits seem to express more of the individuality of the subject. Another thing to remember is that in most every instance there is one side of the subject's face that will

Give young children something interesting to do and you will get natural, unposed pictures. Older children and grown-ups can assume a position to your liking as in the pictures on the opposite page.

photograph better than the other, so when possible, determine this point before placing your subject in front of the Kodak.

Whether the portrait shall be full face, three-quarter or profile will be determined, of course, by the viewpoint from which the subject shows to the best advantage, though you will doubtless make several pictures of a subject from different positions.

FEATURES

With persons having fairly regular features and good complexions it frequently happens that good portraits can be obtained from almost any angle, but in most cases you will find it necessary to subdue some feature or strongly accentuate others to produce the best effect.

As an example, take a young man with very prominent ears; it is obvious in this case that the full face would be displeasing, so, turn the face slowly away from the light until the ear nearest the light disappears from the line of sight.

Sometimes the chin is a little weak; tilting the head slightly upward will help, or the chin can be rested on the hand—a profile, of course, is not to be considered. Double chins can be treated in the same way.

Now take a subject with a massive lower jaw; place him squarely facing the Kodak and you will note that the head outline is nearly rectangular. Request him to turn his head slowly away from the light, and stop at the point where the head outline presents an oval form; it may also be necessary to tilt the head up or down a trifle to produce the most satisfactory view.

When the subject has a very thin face or high cheek bones, the light should be so directed upon the face as to fall just below the point of the cheek bone; this may be easily accomplished by lowering the window shade, blocking the window a little or moving the subject just a trifle farther from the light.

121

Bald pates are easy; have someone hold a sheet of cardboard over the head between the light and the bright spot, just out of lens range.

WATCH THE EYES

You quite often encounter a subject with deep set eyes, or wish to make a picture with the hat shadowing the face. In such cases, to afford sufficient illumination to the eyes, you must turn the subject more toward the light or use a supplementary reflector.

Particular attention should always be paid to the eyes, as the entire facial expression depends so much upon them. Have them in good focus, and avoid double "catch lights," those little points of light.

GLASSES

When eyeglasses are worn, be very particular to see that the glasses do not show a blur from reflected light. If the glasses do show a blur when viewed with your own head directly in front of the camera lens, turn the sitter's face slightly either way, until the blur vanishes.

THE HANDS

Watch the hands carefully and do not have them too far forward from the body or they will then photograph out of proportion with the face. The hand partially closed usually presents a better appearance than when clenched or with fingers extended.

Be careful, too, with the seated figure that an arm or leg is not extended too far forward, especially when making close-ups.

THE FULL LENGTH FIGURE

When portraying the full figure, you naturally have a few more things to consider than when making close-ups. Watch for example, the position of the feet and remember that curves, not angles, make for beauty and harmony. A glass paneled door helps to illuminate the full figure.

DON'T FUSS

If the figure is to be seated, simply request the subject to sit down, and you will usually find that a quick pat here and there will get rid of any ungainly angles—if not, stop right there and invent some excuse to have the subject stand up for a moment, and then again be seated—it doesn't take much to bore even the most willing subject.

PICTURING THE ROOMS OF THE
HOME BY DAYLIGHT

Your staircase may make a good subject.

When making pictures in and about the home we should not overlook photographing the rooms in which we live. It is probably because these pictures can be made at almost any time that we are likely to postpone making them, and the rooms may be newly decorated, furnished or remodeled before we realize that no pictures were taken, showing them as they were before the changes were made.

Few people who have reached middle age have any pictures that show the interior of their childhood home and they keenly realize how imperfectly memory can recall many details which only pictures accurately and permanently record.

The interior of a living room will need a time exposure since the light is so much weaker indoors than under the open sky. As pictures of interiors are made with the camera reasonably close to the subject, some objects only a few feet away, while others are several feet from the lens, a small stop opening must usually be employed to obtain sufficient sharpness or definition in everything.

The furniture of a room should be left as far as possible in its usual place and the room photographed from two or more viewpoints. If a

Medium colored walls and a variety of tones in the furnishings. 20 seconds, f.22, lens focused at 15 feet.

room is to be photographed from one position only, the temptation is to crowd much furniture into a small space. This should always be avoided, as the picture will be far more pleasing if it suggests the comforts of a living room rather than one that is overcrowded.

There should, whenever possible, be enough clear space between the lens and the nearest piece of furniture so that only the floor can be seen in the immediate foreground, at least in the center part of the picture. The reasons for this are that any object which is very close to the camera will appear unduly large in comparison with objects that are farther away, and it will be impossible to include the whole of a large object within the picture area.

To photograph interiors the camera must be placed on a solid table or other rigid support. An adjustable tripod is ideal and the Optipod referred to on page 50 is convenient. The camera should be placed low enough so that more of the floor than the ceiling can

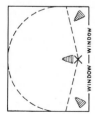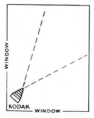

Diagrams show suitable camera positions when making interiors.

124

be seen in the finder. If the picture shows more ceiling than floor it will look topheavy. Avoid, if possible, reflections from glass covered pictures on the walls. Such reflections can frequently be avoided by drawing down one of the window shades, or by tilting the picture slightly.

When the room is dark in tone, the outlines of the furnishings may not be seen clearly in the finder. So while adjusting the camera—not during exposure—have someone hold a lighted candle or household flashlight near the wall. As the light will show brightly in the finder, the outlines of the area that will be included in the picture can be accurately determined.

In the smaller rooms that have but one window, a reflector (a sheet thrown over a screen will do) may be needed to increase the illumination in the corners. If the camera is placed as shown in the right hand diagram, bottom of page 124, for photographing the corner that is

EXPOSURE TABLE FOR INTERIORS

For stop *f*.16 (U. S. 16), or the second stop with single, Double, Diway and Twindar lens cameras. *Double* the exposures with each *smaller* stop, and *halve* the exposures (with some exceptions) with each *larger* stop.	*Bright sun*	*Hazy sun*	*Cloudy bright*	*Cloudy dull*
White walls and more than one window.	4 secs.	10 secs.	20 secs.	40 secs.
White walls and only one window.	6 secs.	15 secs.	30 secs.	1 min.
Medium colored walls and furnishings and more than one window.	8 secs.	20 secs.	40 secs.	1 min. 20 secs.
Medium colored walls and furnishings and only one window.	12 secs.	30 secs.	1 min.	2 mins.
Dark colored walls and furnishings and more than one window.	20 secs.	40 secs.	1 min. 20 secs.	2 mins. 40 secs.
Dark colored walls and furnishings and only one window.	40 secs.	1 min. 20 secs.	2 mins. 40 secs.	5 mins. 20 secs.

These exposures are for rooms where windows get the direct light from the sky and for hours from three hours after sunrise until three hours before sunset. If earlier or later the exposures must be longer.

The fireplace section of the room is always an attractive picture subject. Page 127 tells about photographing against windows and glass paneled doors, as in picture below. These pictures are from Verichrome Film negatives.

diagonally opposite the camera, a reflector of white cloth or paper, about the size of an ordinary window shade, placed as in the diagram, will improve the illumination.

Rooms with two or more windows on one side can be lighted without the aid of a reflector. Such rooms can easily be photographed from various viewpoints. The diagram at the left (page 124) shows that with the camera at position X a series of pictures can be made which will include the area through which the dotted curved line passes. "Shooting" from either corner may also be done, as indicated in this diagram.

The diagram in the center (page 124) shows a good position for the camera when photographing an interior with windows on two sides. With the camera in the position suggested, there will be no need for a reflector.

Interiors are usually photographed by the light that comes through windows on which the sun is not shining. They can also be photographed by the light that comes through windows on which the sun is shining but it is best to subdue the sunlight by placing muslin or cheesecloth screens over the windows, if curtains do not diffuse the light; then double the exposures given in the table on page 125.

126

The illustrations here and the one on page 124 are from photographs that were made by this

Bright day, light diffused by curtains. 2 minutes, f.22. Window and door shades were drawn except for the last 5 seconds of the exposure.

method. The rooms were photographed on days of bright sunshine.
The only change made in the arrangement of the rooms was the
removal of furniture that was too near the camera.

The view at the bottom of page 126 was, for example, made at 10
a.m. The walls, ceiling, and woodwork were all light colored. In addition to the light coming through the paneled door and from windows
in the adjoining room, illumination
was furnished by three windows to the
left and one window behind the camera. The shades on the double-paneled
door and window shown in the picture
were drawn except for the last 5 seconds of the exposure time which was 2
minutes at stop $f.22$. This is important
when photographing towards windows
and glass-paneled doors.

The secret of success lies in controlling the light by raising or lowering the
window shades and opening or closing
doors so the light will be as uniform as
possible in those parts of the room that
are to be photographed, and in always
having the strongest light come from
behind the camera or from any one or
more sides excepting that side of the
room toward which the lens is pointed.
It is also necessary to give an exposure
that is long enough for recording detail
in all but the darkest shadows.

10 *seconds, stop* $f.11$.

INTERIORS
OF PUBLIC BUILDINGS

Public buildings offer great opportunities for attractive interior pictures.
Marble architectural construction in the shape of winding staircases
and balconies, and elaborately carved doors with diffused, indirect
lighting, provide subjects unsurpassed for stately curves and softly
graduated shadows.

127

Time exposures must usually be made, though with a fast lens and good light, slow snapshot exposures will often yield good negatives. The correct exposure in large, softly lighted interiors usually ranges from ten seconds to one minute with a medium size stop, say $f.11$. During longer exposures many persons may pass in front of the camera without registering a blur on the film. But if only a ten or twenty second exposure is required it is better to close and open the shutter if persons in front of the camera do not move out of the range of view of your lens, meanwhile keeping careful tab on the fleeting second hand.

Except where the effect of light through a window is desired, the picture can be taken just as well at night. Soft, shaded lights a fair distance away will do no harm with a film having the non-halation quality as in Verichrome, "SS" Pan, and Panatomic Films.

The combination of a daytime interior scene with the view afforded

through a window or door, correctly exposing the whole, is seldom achieved except by a combination daylight and flashlight exposure, with a Photoflash Lamp. Interesting pictures can be made by shooting through fancy grilled windows and doorways with an exposure to fit *outdoor* conditions. A small stop, about $f.16$, to yield the necessary depth of field will give a picture showing the outside scene with the grill work in delightful silhouette pattern.

Suitable buildings for interior pictures are libraries, railroad terminals, city halls, courthouses, and museums.

Don't let the beams of sunlight fool you; exposure should be sufficient to record some shadow detail. 1 *second at stop* $f.16$.

128

OUTDOOR PICTURES AT NIGHT

THERE is something about pictures made outdoors at night that arouses the imagination and fascinates one. They are often pictures of ordinary subjects made under unusual conditions, and are therefore more interesting than the usual type of picture made by daylight.

A novel idea for your collection would be to make two pictures of a building or a street scene, one by daylight and the other at night, both pictures being made from exactly the same position—the comparison would be most interesting.

Pictures made after dark of buildings with their myriads of brilliantly lighted windows, reflections in water and from wet pavements, campfire scenes and fireworks, remind one of fantastic scenes such as described in fairy books.

Reflections on wet pavements often add interest and aid composition. 8 minutes, f.16 for this.

A large industrial plant like a steel mill or a blast furnace will offer excellent opportunities to make unusual pictures at night. The flying sparks from the chimneys and the bright light reflected on the smoke will prove most effective. City skylines, especially across a body of water which reflects the lights, are striking.

Such pictures can be made with any kind of camera with a "time"

129

exposure adjustment. Naturally, for time exposures the camera must be placed on a tripod or some convenient solid support.

While splendid outdoor night pictures can be made on Verichrome Film, Kodak "SS" Pan Film is the ideal negative material for this work as it permits a much shorter exposure and is sensitive to lights of all colors. For miniature cameras taking the same film as the Kodak Retina, the new Super X Film will again cut down the exposure time. As in "SS" Pan Film, a special dye on the back prevents halation.

Kodak Panatomic Film is also a halation-proof film and sensitive to all colors, though it is not as fast as "SS" Pan.

LIGHTED STREETS AND PUBLIC SQUARES

The "White Way" or theater district of a large city offers bright scenes

A 4 minute exposure at stop f.4.5. Kodak Verichrome Film.

that would make an attractive souvenir collection, and the town or village square with its corner churches and soldiers' monument, is well worth an exposure, especially on a wet night when the pavement shows interesting reflections. Snow also adds considerably to the attractiveness of such views. Note picture on page 229.

In estimating the exposure necessary it is not so much the lights within the picture area as the general illumination that is important. The pictorial effect may sometimes be improved considerably, by including some of the lights.

The pictures will not show any trace of occasional passing vehicles or pedestrians during the long exposures necessary with most cameras. If an automobile or trolley car approaches, the shutter should be closed or your hand placed momentarily in front of the lens, as any moving bright lights will show as streaks in the negative. Exposure will necessarily depend on the quantity and quality of the light and the size of the stop opening. With stop $f.8$ (U.S. 4) or $f.11$ (U.S. 8) an exposure of from one second to one minute for a well lighted subject will give very satisfactory results with "SS" Pan Film. With Verichrome or Panatomic Film the exposure must be increased about twice.

Cameras with large aperture lenses permit making slow *snapshots* at night with "SS" Pan Film. Slightly faster shutter speeds may be used with the Retina and other miniature cameras loaded with Super X Pan Film. You have perhaps already studied the groups of pictures on pages 16, 17, 18, 19, which give an idea of the widening field of possibilities as lens apertures widen. The pictures clearly indicate that the fast lens is indeed the versatile lens.

The picture of the fountain in front of the Electrical Building at

Printed from two negatives; one for the moon exposed 2 seconds, one for the scene exposed 20 minutes after moon was hidden by tree foliage.

Twenty minutes exposure at lens aperture f.22.

Wet streets add interest. Three minutes, f.16.

Night beach parties can easily be taken with Photoflash.

A fifteen minute exposure at stop f.8 will get pictures of this kind where good illumination is furnished by street lamps.

Ten minutes at f.11. Camera must, of course, be on solid support for "time" exposures.

Camp life at night easily recorded with Photoflash.

Night sports can be caught with Photoflash which can be used with a synchronizer on a rapid shutter if action is very great.

A real moonlight picture. Exposure 45 minutes, f.16 stop.

...scinated by a flashlight played along the shore line. Photoflash "shot" from the canoe caught him.

Made from a boat twenty feet from shore. Flash powder in a paper, tied on the stick, was ignited by the campfire.

the Century of Progress Fair in Chicago, shown on this page, was made on "SS" Film, exposure 3 minutes with stop 16.

FLOODLIGHTED BUILDINGS

More and more public buildings are being illuminated after dark, and their beauty shown off to great advantage by the powerful, indirect lights that bathe them in soft light. Here, indeed, are chances for unusual architectural studies. There are probably some floodlighted buildings in your own town or city that you will want to take. In the big cities there are many opportunities. The Capitol at Washington, for instance, is beautifully displayed after dark and can be easily photographed with exposures of two to three minutes with "SS" Film and stop 16, or four to six minutes with Verichrome or Panatomic Film. Note the picture of it on page 129.

Use a tripod or other firm support for the camera and work from a position where there is not too much movement or obstruction near the

Fountains, shafts of light, and silhouetted foliage contribute to fantastic designs for night pictures. 3 minutes, stop f.16, "SS" Film.

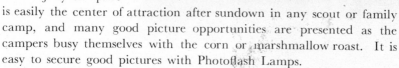

lens. Street lights must be kept as far out of the immediate foreground as possible where the building itself is the thing you are after.

THE CAMPFIRE

The jolly campfire is easily the center of attraction after sundown in any scout or family camp, and many good picture opportunities are presented as the campers busy themselves with the corn or marshmallow roast. It is easy to secure good pictures with Photoflash Lamps.

The method is quite simple. Set up your camera on a tripod to include the view desired. To determine the area which will be included in your picture, someone can hold a flashlight, match, or firebrand at the right and left boundaries of the group, while the photographer is looking in the finder. Use stop *f*.11 (U.S. 8), or No. 1, or the largest stop opening on a box camera.

To one side and slightly behind the camera, hold a Photo*flash* Lamp,

in its reflector, (see page 142) about five feet from the ground. Now open the shutter of your camera, press the button to set off the Photoflash,

Real moonlight. Full moon, clear night, snow, exposure 15 minutes, stop opening f.8.

135

then close the shutter. Before setting off the flash, see that no one is staring at the camera, as this is likely to spoil the story interest of the picture.

As mentioned on page 146, there are two sizes of Photoflash lamps for average use. Where large areas are to be included use Photoflash Lamp No. 75. There are battery-contained reflector units that accommodate more than one Photoflash.

FIRES AT NIGHT

Fascinating as day photographs of fires are with their volume of swirling smoke, the night picture of a building afire has a picturesqueness of its own. While such chances do not occur very often, they are wholly worth the effort to picture them and for these and other opportunities that present themselves infrequently it is well to always have your camera loaded and ready.

A big fire, whether it rages in the light of day or during the hours of darkness, presents an ever changing scene and you never can tell when or where the next spectacular sight will be.

At night both sky and landscape are dark and you can not photograph dark smoke against a dark background. You can, however, get silhouette effects. This can usually be done when the flames are brightly outlined against the darkness by giving an exposure of 2 or 3 seconds with a large stop opening. When making exposures with a box camera, always use the largest stop. Do not hold the camera in your hands, place it on some firm support or a tripod.

Red and orange are the predominating colors of fire; therefore, the best results will be obtained if your camera is loaded with a film having a panchromatic emulsion, as such film is sensitive to *all* colors. Verichrome will also give good results but requires a little longer exposure.

FIREWORKS

Fireworks, too, offer opportunities for beautiful and novel pictures. The effect wanted is of streams of light with the incidental sparks caught in the slower-moving showers. These lines fall beautifully, tracing graceful patterns that make splendid studies.

Since the film is not affected by a dark sky, the shutter may remain open or be reopened to capture successive bursts. The lens must point towards an unobstructed part of the sky in order to get a solid background, and you must be prepared to close the shutter should any spectators get too close to the lens. Many brilliant bursts can be secured with an exposure of one second and as long as they are not set on stationary pieces attached to a framework, the camera can be tilted as much as necessary to get the picture area fairly well filled. Simply aim the camera at the space where the displays are being set off and you will not fail to get some striking pictures. The camera must be on a firm support when making pictures of set pieces that are on the ground, and where buildings are included, as shown in the illustration on this page; otherwise the camera may safely be held in the hands.

LIGHTNING

Lightning is in somewhat the same class as fireworks and what you should aim to get are brilliant ribbons or streaks of light against a black sky background. The most satisfactory method is to place the camera on a tripod at an open window pointed in the direction of

Exposure 45 seconds, stop f.8, Kodak "SS" Pan Film.

137

Exposure 5 minutes with stop f.11 (U. S. 8), Kodak "SS" Pan Film.

the last few flashes. The shutter, set at "time" and using the largest opening, is left open, and closed after a single flash, or left open for several flashes (see picture page 139).

The only form of lightning that does not picture satisfactorily is sheet lightning, which uniformly illuminates a broad expanse of sky. With this kind of lightning, however, interesting silhouettes of trees and buildings can often be secured from a good vantage point. The brilliant zig-zag lines of chain lightning give the most spectacular effects.

The camera can be held in the hands for photographing lightning, with the shutter set for "time." It is perhaps best that the film be turned to a new section after each flash so as not to show more than one big streak.

"BY THE LIGHT OF THE SILVERY MOON"

Moonlight will make pictures just as sunlight does, but as it is a great many times weaker than sunlight, exposures must be very considerably increased. Perhaps the simplest way to calculate a moonlight exposure is to give 25 minutes for each 1/100 second exposure that would be given for

A pseudo moonlight picture, 1/100 second, f.8, just before sunset.

138

the same scene by sunlight. For example, the exposure in bright sunlight for a landscape with a dark-toned object in the immediate foreground would be 1/25 with stop *f*.11 or U.S. 8.   Then the exposure by
the light of a full moon would be 100 minutes with the same stop.
This could be cut down to 50 minutes with stop *f*.8 or U. S. 4. For
a landscape without a dark-toned object in the immediate foreground
about 25 minutes with *f*.8 or U. S. 4 would be ample; for distant landscapes the exposure can be from 10 to 15 minutes. If the ground is
covered with snow, shorter exposures can be made; see illustrations,
pages 132, 133 and 135.

If a daylight effect is desired, these exposures must be multiplied by
4 and this applies only to nights when the sky is clear and the moon is
full. The half moon does not give even half as much light as a full moon.

With a single lens and all fixed focus cameras, use the largest stop
and double the exposures given above. These suggestions apply only
to pictures made by moonlight and not those showing the moon itself.

PSEUDO MOONLIGHT PICTURES

Attractive "moonlight" scenes can be made by sunlight. This is best
done during the sunset hour and when there are masses of clouds
floating in the western sky which create lighting conditions favorable
for picturing "moonlight" scenes by sunlight. The sun can be wholly

or partially obscured and if the
light is red, yellow, or orange
a snapshot exposure with a
medium stop opening can be
given.   To secure a night effect from a negative exposed
in such a manner, it must be
printed long enough so that all
but the highlights will be dark.
Notice the pseudo moonlight
shot on page 138.

For lightning point camera at sky, open
shutter when set for a "time" exposure,
close shutter after a flash or flashes.

139

MIRROR PICTURES *are intriguing. When focusing, for reflected images only, it is necessary to add distance from mirror to subject to distance from mirror to lens and set the focus accordingly.*

If it is desired to include the subject itself *in the picture and get it, as well as the reflected image, reasonably sharp, the focus should be set for the distance from the mirror to the lens. The smaller the lens opening the greater the depth of field and the sharper will be both images. Naturally, the nearer the subject is*

to the mirror the less is required in the matter of "depth."

In the picture above, the subjects were about two feet from the mirror and the camera was six feet from the mirror. As both subject and reflected image were to be included in the picture the focus was set at six feet. Stop 16 was used and Photoflash furnished the light.

If the figures and camera were in a position to show only the reflected *image in the picture being taken the focus would then have been set at the eight-foot distance mark.*

140

SNAPSHOTS INDOORS AT NIGHT

Any camera that can be loaded with Kodak "SS" Pan Film may now be used to take snapshots indoors at night by artificial light. This includes box Brownies and most other single and doublet lens cameras, as well as the most versatile of Kodaks. In addition to the camera and the film, you need only two or three Mazda Photoflood Lamps and suitable reflectors.

Photoflood Lamps fit all regular lamp sockets, and are good for many pictures. When lighted they literally flood the subject with picture-taking "sunshine." There are two sizes for the amateur, designated as the No. 1 and the No. 2. The No. 2 gives twice the light and has three times the life of the No. 1.

1/25 second, stop f.6.3. Two No. 1 Photofloods in Kodaflector at "A." One No. 1 Photoflood in home lamp at "B." Lamps about 4 and 5 feet from subject. "SS" Pan Film.

To make snapshots with box cameras, and other single and doublet lens cameras, you need two or three No. 2 Photofloods in Kodak Handy Reflectors, or similar reflector units.

Cameras with f.6.3 or faster lenses can make snapshots with No. 1 Photofloods in reflectors. If No. 2 Photofloods are used, however, with the

ALL YOU NEED

Any Camera that can be loaded with Kodak "SS" Pan Film.

A Few Photoflood Lamps.

A Roll of Kodak "SS" Pan Film.

141

SNAPSHOTS

with any camera and No. 2
Photofloods. With f.6.3 or
faster lens camera use No. 1 or
No. 2 Photofloods. Replace
regular bulbs and shades of
home lamps with Photofloods
and Kodak Handy Reflectors.
Load camera with Kodak "SS"
Pan Film.

QUICK TIME
EXPOSURES

with any camera having a
"Time" adjustment. Use No. 1
or No. 2 Photofloods. Replace
bulbs in home lamps with
Photofloods, with or without
reflectors. Load camera with
Kodak "SS" Pan Film, Panatomic, or Verichrome Film.

PHOTOFLASH
PICTURES

with any camera having a
"Time" adjustment. Use either No. 10 or No. 20 Photoflash
bulb. Equip any home lamp
with a Photoflash bulb and
Kodak Handy Reflector, or use
a Portable Reflector Unit as
shown at right.

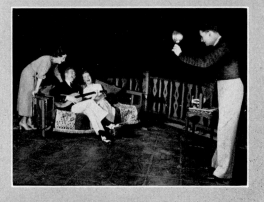

faster lens cameras, you may use a more rapid shutter speed to stop action, or a smaller diaphragm opening to secure a greater range of sharpness throughout the picture.

Kodak "SS" Pan Film is, as previously mentioned, completely color-sensitive and its speed makes it especially adapted for making night snapshots and other indoor pictures.

BOX BROWNIE, SINGLE AND DOUBLET LENS CAMERAS

To take a snapshot indoors at night with a box Brownie, or most other single or doublet lens cameras, load the camera with Kodak "SS" Pan Film. Select a room with light colored walls, and arrange two bridge type lamps as shown in the illustration below, one three feet, the other four feet from the subject. Replace the shades of the lamps with the inexpensive cardboard Kodak Handy Reflectors. Place one No. 2 Mazda Photoflood bulb in each of the lamps. Frame your subject in either the vertical or horizontal finder of the camera. Use the largest diaphragm or stop opening. Hold the camera steady and press the shutter lever. Cameras with adjustable shutter speeds should be set to take the picture at 1/25 second.

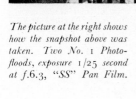

F.6.3 AND FASTER LENS CAMERAS

Cameras with *f*.6.3 or faster lenses, loaded with "SS" Pan Film, can take the picture shown at the left with two No. 1 Photofloods in reflectors.

143

The picture at the right shows how the snapshot above was taken. Two No. 1 Photofloods, exposure 1/25 second at f.6.3, "SS" Pan Film.

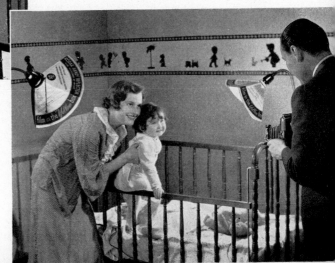

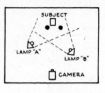

Brownie camera snap-shot, largest stop opening. "SS" Pan Film. Two No. 2 Photofloods in Kodak Handy Reflectors, one 3 and one 4 ft. from subject.

With the diaphragm set at $f.6.3$ snap the picture at a speed no faster than 1/25 second.

If two No. 2 Photofloods in reflectors are used, however, the picture can be taken at 1/50 second with an $f.6.3$ opening, or at 1/25 second with an $f.11$ opening.

TIME EXPOSURES

Any camera that can be set for "Time" can take time exposures of subjects with either No. 1 or No. 2 Photofloods. Place the camera on a solid support. Frame subject in finder. With shutter set for "Time," press lever once to open lens; and again after the exposure to close the lens. The length of time the lens should be left open to take the picture depends upon the kind of film used, number of lights and type of reflectors, and the distance the lamps are from the subject. With "SS" Pan Film and two No. 1 Photofloods in home lamps with regular reflectors 5 to 10 feet from the subject, make an exposure of one-half to two seconds at stop $f.8$. Double the exposure time if Verichrome or Panatomic Film is used.

PHOTOFLOOD TIME EXPOSURES OF ROOM INTERIORS

144   When Photofloods are used in ceiling or wall lamps for general illumi-

One No. 1 Photoflood in reflector at "A"; two No. 1 Photofloods in lamp with large shade at "B," 5 ft. from subject. Stop $f.4.5$, 1/50 sec. "SS" Pan Film.

nation to take time exposures of room interiors, a much longer exposure time is required than for taking close-ups with lights in reflectors held close to the subject. Color of furnishings, for example, and tone of the wall paper must be taken into consideration as well as the kind of film used, reflectors, and number of lights. If in doubt as to the proper exposure, it is suggested that you take two pictures of the same subject, allowing twice as long an exposure time for the second picture as for the first.

HELPFUL HINTS

For more pleasing pictures with Photofloods, especially close-ups, lamps should be placed on each side of the subject, and closer to the subject on one side than on the other. At least one lamp should be a foot higher than the subject's head. If Photofloods are used on only one side, be sure to place something on the other side of the subject to reflect light onto the shadowed side. A sheet or large white towel thrown over a screen or high-backed chair will do.

Where home lamps are used with the regular shades, tip them to direct the light onto the subject. If this is not possible, remove the shades and hold some sort of reflector *back* of the bare lamps to throw the light forward. A white cardboard will help.

It is best to complete all preliminaries with the ordinary bulbs in the home lamps, then when all is in readiness, replace them with Photoflood bulbs. With focusing cameras, get the distance right. If, for example, you have focused for six feet, be sure that the distance from the subject to the lens is just six feet. Better measure it.

No. 2 Photoflood in reflector at "A," 5 ft. from subject.
No. 1 Photoflood in reflector at "B," 4 ft. from subject.
Stop f.8. 1/10 sec.
"SS" Pan Film.

CAUTION: *Photoflood Lamps, especially the No. 2 size, become quite hot and should not be permitted to come into contact with the fabric of shades on home lamps, or other inflammable materials.*

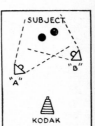

145

SELF TIMER

By clipping a Kodak Self Timer to the cable release of your camera, you, too, can be in the picture when snapshots or other automatic exposures are made with Photoflood Lamps. A Kodak Portrait Attachment or a Diffusion Portrait Attachment placed over the regular camera lens permits making pictures at arm's length from subject, and will give big images or "close-ups" of your subjects.

PHOTOFLASH PICTURES

For night pictures where it is not convenient or practical to use Photofloods, use the Mazda Photo*flash* bulb. This bulb gives an instantaneous *flash* of light (about 1/50 second). It is good for one picture. No noise, no flame, no smoke. Fits any home lamp socket, or may be used in portable reflector containing flashlight batteries.

Set the camera for "Time," and place it on a solid support. Press shutter lever to open lens, flash the bulb, and press shutter lever to close lens. Use largest stop on single or doublet lens cameras.

Photo*flash* bulbs No. 10 and No. 20 are for cameras that do not have focal plane shutters. If used with a Kodak Handy Reflector, the smaller bulb will be found satisfactory for most indoor shots. Hold about 10 feet from subject.

When using Photoflash indoors, bright room lights near subject should not be on, or a secondary image may be recorded if the subject moves, before or after the flash, when the camera shutter is open.

Photoflash bulb in reflector, 8 ft. from subject. Camera 10 ft. Stop f.8. "SS" Pan Film.

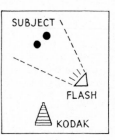

146

Made with No. 10 Photoflash Lamp in Kodak Handy Reflector; 10 feet, stop f.11. Verichrome Film negative.

EXPOSURE TABLE FOR NO. 10 PHOTOFLASH LAMP

With the No. 20 Photoflash Lamp, use next smaller opening

For Kodak Super Sensitive Panchromatic Film.

For Panatomic or Verichrome Film use next larger opening.

Distance Lamp to Subject	Diaphragm or Stop Opening		
	*One Photoflash in Kodak Handy Reflector	One Photoflash in Ordinary Reflector	One Photoflash Without Reflector
20 feet	f.6.3	f.4.5	
15 feet	f.11	f.6.3	f.4.5
10 feet	f.16	f.11	f.6.3
6 feet	f.22	f.16	f.11

*If a Kodaflector is used, give one half the exposure indicated above for the Kodak Handy Reflector.

A white card held directly behind a bare Photoflash Lamp will enable you to use the diaphragms recommended for ordinary reflector.

With box, single lens or doublet lens cameras, use the largest stop opening and use the distances given for f.16 or f.11.

147

Taken with Kodak Bantam Special on Pana- *an idea of what can be accomplished indoors*
tomic Film; 1/50 second, f.3.5, two No. 1 *with a fast-lens miniature camera and a couple*
Photofloods. This appealing baby picture gives *of Photoflood Lamps.*

KODAFLECTOR THE IDEAL LIGHTING UNIT

Much light is lost from lack of proper reflecting surfaces around light bulbs when they are used in room lamps and fixtures. The Kodaflector increases the intensity of the light from Photoflood Lamps several times. With this lighting unit, indoor pictures are made much more easily. The room's regular lighting arrangement need not be disturbed.

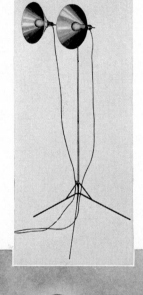

The Kodaflector also increases the light intensity of the Photo*flash* Lamp considerably.

The telescopic standard and the reflectors of the Kodaflector are light in weight and sturdily constructed. The reflectors are of polished, lacquered aluminum, are equipped with a 12-foot extension cord and can be used separately.

AT RIGHT: *The convenient Kodaflector which increases the efficiency of lights several times.*
BELOW: *The Kodaflector is shown in use, and below at right is a picture made at the time.*

149

Special adapters are required to give full efficiency when the No. 2 Photoflood Lamps are used.

KODAFLECTOR DIFFUSER

The Diffuser softens the light from the Kodaflector giving better quality in portrait studies, and is of particular advantage when using Kodachrome. Exposure must be increased according to instuctions furnished.

EXPOSURE TABLE for Kodak Super Sensitive Panchromatic Film and Two Photoflood Lamps
When using Kodak Panatomic or Verichrome Film double the exposure.

Distance Lamps to Subject	Diaphragm or Stop Opening	Exposure in Seconds				
		†No. 1 Photoflood Lamps in Kodak Handy Reflectors	†No. 2 Photoflood Lamps in Kodak Handy Reflectors	*No. 1 Photoflood Lamps in Ordinary Reflectors	No. 1 Photoflood Lamps without Reflectors	No. 2 Photoflood Lamps without Reflectors
4 feet	$f.4.5$	1/50	1/100	1/25	1/10	1/25
"	$f.6.3$	1/25	1/50	1/10	1/5	1/10
"	$f.11$(U.S.8)	1/10	1/25	1/5	1/2	1/5
"	$f.16$	1/5	1/10	1/2	1	1/2
6 feet	$f.4.5$	1/25	1/50	1/10	1/5	1/10
"	$f.6.3$	1/10	1/25	1/5	1/2	1/5
"	$f.11$(U.S.8)	1/5	1/10	1/2	1	1/2
"	$f.16$	1/2	1/5	1	2	1
10 feet	$f.4.5$	1/10	1/25	1/5	1/2	1/5
"	$f.6.3$	1/5	1/10	1/2	1	1/2
"	$f.11$(U.S.8)	1/2	1/5	1	2	1
"	$f.16$	1	1/2	2	4	2

†If Kodaflectors are used give one-half the exposure indicated above for the Kodak Handy Reflector.
*With No. 2 Photoflood Lamps the exposure should be one-half or two-thirds of the exposure given for No. 1 Lamps, depending upon kind of reflector.
This table is for portraits and light-colored interiors. For dark-colored interiors without people and for dark clothing, double the above exposures. If 1/10 second is given, using 1/5 second will double the exposure time.
Doubling the number of lamps will halve the exposure.
When the lamps are used for general illumination to make a picture of a room, use stop $f.16$ (U.S. 16) to get sufficient depth or range of sharpness.
With box, single lens or doublet lens cameras, use the largest stop opening and use the exposures shown above for $f.16$ or $f.11$.
NOTE: Do not use more than five No. 1 Photoflood Lamps on a single fused circuit; if six lamps or more are required, be sure to use different circuits. Do not use more than three No. 2 Photoflood Lamps on a single fused circuit.

ORDINARY LAMPS

If, in an emergency, you want to take pictures at night but find that you have no special lamps or reflectors on hand, then make time exposures using regular home service lamps.

Use enough lamps to total 350 watts, placing about 250 watts on one side of the camera axis and 100 watts on the other, but all lamps at the same distance from the subject.

EXPOSURE TABLE using Regular Service Lamps without Reflectors (350-watt total) for Kodak Super Sensitive Panchromatic Film

When using Kodak Panatomic Film double the exposure.
With Kodak Verichrome Film give four times the exposure.

Distance Lamps to Subject	Diaphragm or Stop Opening	Exposure in Seconds
4 feet	*f*.4.5	½
"	*f*.6.3	1
"	*f*.11	2
"	*f*.16	4
10 feet	*f*.4.5	2
"	*f*.6.3	4
"	*f*.11	8
"	*f*.16	16

This table is for portraits and light-colored interiors. For dark-colored interiors without people, double the above exposures.

With box, single lens or doublet lens cameras, use the largest stop opening and use the exposures shown above for *f*.16 or *f*.11.

INTERIORS BY ORDINARY ELECTRIC LIGHTS

City homes are sometimes so close to other buildings that it is not always possible to get enough illumination to photograph some of the rooms by daylight. When electric light is available this difficulty is overcome. By using plugs that will hold two, three or four lamps and connecting with the nearest floor or ceiling outlet, any quantity of light can be placed where it is needed. The regular wall and ceiling lights will often supply enough illumination, or if more light is needed lamps of higher wattage can be used. By using the Kodak Handy Reflector or a Kodaflector, the illumination is increased considerably.

The illustration on page 152 shows a kitchen and dining alcove photo-

151

One 60-watt lamp in an amber shade in dining alcove. One 100-watt lamp in ceiling over sink. One 40-watt lamp in ceiling over camera. Exposure 15 seconds with stop f.11 (U. S. 8). Kodak Super Sensitive Panchromatic Film.

graphed by a single 60-watt lamp in an amber shade over the table, a 100-watt lamp in a porcelain shade over the sink, and a 40-watt lamp in the ceiling over the camera. The exposure was 15 seconds with stop f.11 (U. S. 8); larger rooms with dark wall paper and hangings would of course need more illumination and longer exposure. Each room will call for its own exposure, but it will soon be found comparatively easy to estimate a satisfactory exposure.

Lighted floor and table lamps can be photographed in their normal positions and will not fog the picture if the bulbs do not show through or under the shade. They photograph much more attractively when lighted and can improve many an interior picture.

A distinction must be made between lamps that show in the picture area and those that do not show but are used for illumination. Brilliant pictures by artificial light can be made only when the light from the lamps that are not in the picture is prevented from shining directly into the lens while the exposure is being made. A magazine or newspaper can be so held as to shade the lens from direct light.

"CONTEMPLATION"

Taken from just the right angle and height to include an interesting pattern of shadows, well balanced by sun-lighted portions, all of which form a perfect stage setting for the lone actor . . . the cat.

In making the enlargement a bit of "dodging" was required to accentuate the checkered design in part of the pavement. The shadow sections were printed deep for a correct feeling of division

of tone masses, light and dark, which almost entirely make up this fine photograph.

Such technique is often necessary to provide a print that merits exhibition in a salon.

The author of the picture evidently has trained himself to see the artistic in the commonplace.

A Panatomic Film negative made with a miniature Kodak, 1/50 second, stop f.11.

"Contemplation"

STUNT PICTURES

May his better self win.

Most cameras are much too well behaved. Let them have their fling. Even the simplest camera is really a versatile instrument, capable of tricks providing entertainment for the most sophisticated picture takers.

For instance, anybody can photograph living people—but imagination is required to photograph ghosts. Students of the supernatural have long debated whether or not spirits can be caught by the camera. Well, there's a chance for the amateur photographer. He may not photograph genuine, air-floating spirits, but perhaps his friends won't be able to prove that the ghostly figure of his picture was not really a spook.

Triplets don't come in many families, yet the prankishly minded photographer can produce three of a kind, or even quintuplets, from any family.

Hollywood regales the public with hair-raising railroad wrecks in scenes that never happen. The home photographer can do the same thing if he has a toy train and a flair for getting interesting and realistic effects on a table top.

SPOOKS!

Ghost photography, for example, is easy enough. Here's the scheme: First you photograph the door, just as if you were "shooting" that and nothing else. Then, without moving the camera or winding the film, dress Brother Bill in a sheet. This entirely material ghost takes up his position at the door, and the picture is snapped again—this time with the shutter set for only half the exposure time required to make the photograph of the door. You see it is just as easy to make a double exposure by meaning to as it is by forgetting to wind the film.

DOUBLE AND TRIPLE EXPOSURE STUNTS

If double exposure on one film can create specters out of nowhere, it shouldn't be difficult by the same means to do all kinds of tricks with living people. Is there a young daughter who is so charming that you would like to have three of her? The Kodak will produce three—in one picture.

First hang up or find a plain, dark background, preferably black, without any markings or wrinkles to distinguish one part from any other part. Dress the child in fairly bright clothes—white, yellow, pink or light blue. Then comes the exposure, not double exposure this time, but triple exposure.

Focus the camera, which must be on a tripod or some other firm support. Have the child sit in front of the background in such a position as to appear toward one side of the finder. Then, with proper lighting, take the picture. Without winding the film, and with care not to move the camera, move the child so that she appears in the center of the finder, and snap the shutter again.

Repeat the same procedure for the other side of the picture. Each exposure should be of the proper length of time to take the picture if no "funny business" were involved. Each placing of the child in the finder should avoid overlapping the space representing an adjoining image.

The result: obviously, triplets having

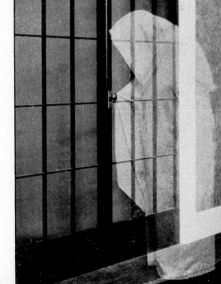

The ghost walks again. The most mystifying pictures are sometimes the simplest to make.

155

"Hear no evil, see no evil, speak no evil." By a perfectly simple technique with a Kodak, this little girl was turned into triplets imitating the famous trio of Oriental monkeys.

their picture taken. If the background is dark and plain, the area of the background in front of which the brightly dressed child sat for the first exposure will not obliterate the figures on the film when the little girl moves over for the later exposures.

There is hardly any limit to the number of tricks that can be done by double exposure or multiple exposure, when photographs are taken against the kind of background described. If the placings of the subject are carefully measured, it is perfectly possible to show one's best friend offering himself a cigaret; or to show him squaring off for a boxing bout with the other half of his "dual personality."

THE MIRROR PICTURE

A mirror is the important "property" in another type of camera stunt that is less deceptive than interesting. The subject of a mirror photograph appears in the picture twice, or even four times—as in a double or multiple exposure—but the sense of wonder on the part of persons seeing the picture gives way to admiration for an attractive and ingenious portrait.

This sort of photograph gets away, naturally, from stiff, "posed" portraiture, and it is refreshing to see—when the camera has been

156

placed in the proper position at one side— a profile of the subject along with a front-face view in the mirror.

Is this difficult? No more difficult than any amateur camera portrait. Only one unusual thing must be kept in mind. In calculating the distance for focusing on the image in the mirror, remember to add the distance between the mirror and the subject's face to the distance between the mirror and the camera's lens, as previously explained in connection with the picture on page 140.

SHADOWS

Remember what fun it was, in childhood, to cast animal shadows on a wall by holding the hands in strange ways in front of a light? Well, there is even more entertainment in doing the same thing for the camera, because then the shadows will "keep."

The stunt can be done indoors, with a Photoflood or a Photoflash lamp, or it can be done out of doors in bright sunlight if the sun is shining from one side. No special technique of the camera is required to make such a photograph except to shoot from the proper angle and use as small a lens opening as the light permits, in order to get both figure and shadow sharply recorded. At the choice of the photographer, the picture may include either just the shadows on a light wall or both the shadows and the person whose hands are making them.

QUEER ANGLE SHOTS

Pictures taken from a position very near the

Four portraits—of one young lady—at one click of the shutter. . . . It's all done by mirrors, but there's no magic about this.

Is it a donkey or camel? No matter—it's an interesting picture for the album.

157

This photograph defies geography and gravity. Where, in space, were the girls, and where was the Kodak? Answer: The girls were leaning over looking down at the Kodak which was placed on the floor. Photofloods furnished the light.

feet or a person with legs extended, looking toward the head, can give very much distorted perspective, with rather shocking results. But a more elaborate trick in unusual angles is done with the camera set on the ground, pointing upward when the sun is not in position to shine into the lens. A group of five or six persons should surround it in a circle, joining their arms, bending over, and looking down. A Kodak Self Timer will click the shutter at the right moment. The picture quite baffles attempts to guess the position in space occupied by the circle of subjects; a human ring seeming to stand nowhere.

One precaution is necessary in taking such a picture outdoors. The group should stand on a white pavement or on a sandy beach on a sunny day, so that light is reflected up into their faces.

TABLE-TOP PHOTOGRAPHY

The way to adventure farthest without leaving home with the Kodak is through table-top picture making.

Would you like a bear-hunting scene in the Rockies to show to friends? A table top, a little toy bear, some gravel, a small stone, two or three small weeds, and a picture of Rocky Mountain scenery clipped from a magazine will pay the fare to a

Toys make interesting table-top studies.

158

ders, when the temperature of the developer is 65 degrees Fahrenheit. Tray developed negatives will be contrasty if a double strength developer is used and development is continued until the background (as seen from the back of the negative) is blackened to the base of the emulsion.

Unless full length figures are to be shown the lower part of a silhouette negative should usually be masked in printing. The mask may be made of any kind of opaque paper, cut or torn to the shape desired. The mask may be laid between the printing paper and the negative, or placed over the back of the negative. If several prints are to be made the mask should be fastened to two of the margins of the negative with gummed paper. The head and shoulder silhouette on page 160 was masked, at the bottom, in this fashion.

Should it happen that anything that was outside of the area covered by the sheet shows in the negative, this may be gotten rid of by applying opaque with a spotting brush (both are furnished by Kodak dealers) to the back of the negative. The outlines of costumes and accessories may also be modified by this method, if desired.

Silhouettes should be printed on a contrasty paper like No. 4 or No. 5 Velox. Any softer grade of paper is not suitable, unless the background part of the negative is extremely dense.

The pictures at the top of page 164 give an idea of what can be

Costume silhouettes are always appealing.

Circular masks were used on the negatives of these clever silhouettes. See details below.

accomplished by applying a little ingenuity in the matter of accessories. Branches of leaves, either artificial or real, may be pinned to the sheet, as may also other things. Still other types of accessories may be suspended from threads as was done in the picture at the left, of the bird on the circular perch. The negatives may be masked to any shape desired; in these pictures the circular form adds much to their attractiveness. Paper objects may be pinned or stuck to the sheet as was done in the silhouette of the juggler, on page 167, and if properly spaced the illusion will be perfect.

SILHOUETTES AT PARTIES

Silhouette pictures present almost endless possibilities and are a welcome novelty at parties, particularly when the guests are in costume, although, as is apparent from several of our illustrations, we do not need to wait for an event such as New Year's, Valentine's Day or Hallowe'en to make attractive silhouettes.

The making of silhouette pictures offers an excellent chance for one to apply ingenuity when making pictures of the story-telling type. The white "Simple Simon" silhouette shows what can be done and the use of the characters in nursery rimes is in itself suggestive. The boy in the picture was sitting on a box. His peaked cap was made out of a newspaper, the fish pole was a limb of a tree with a weight attached to the end of the line so that it was held taut, and the pail is one that was

164

borrowed from the cook. Often accessories of the kind can be represented by cutting them out of cardboard and propping them up from the back. This white silhouette was made by printing from a positive instead of a negative.

To make a positive, place a negative in a printing frame in contact with an Eastman Process Film, which is furnished in cut sheets. This film is capable of giving great contrast—just what is needed in silhouette work. The Process Film is much faster than Velox paper and, consequently, requires a shorter exposure. Try giving an "on-and-off" with a 25-watt electric lamp at, say, a distance of five feet. One or two trials will set you on the right road. The contrast developer that is recommended on the instruction sheet that comes with the film is ideal

for contrasty results, or if you do not care to make up this developer secure a package of Eastman Hydroquinone Developer Powders.

BY DAYLIGHT

Satisfactory silhouettes can be made indoors by daylight, using a window or a glass panelled door as the background. All light in the room should be cut off except that which comes through the door or window in front of which we are going to pose our subject.

Window silhouettes by daylight are easy.

165

To avoid getting detail in the hair on the side of the head toward the camera, pull the shade down so that it is but a few inches from the top of the subject's head.

When an ordinary two-sash window is used as a background, it will be necessary, when the subject is a child, that he sit in a chair or, better still, on a stool or the end of a table, which will raise the figure sufficiently to give more than a head and shoulders effect if desired.

A window should be selected which admits an abundance of unobstructed light.

If a tree or some other dark toned object can be seen from the position of the camera the window will not make a completely white background. The whole theory of silhouette making is the securing of a white background that is much more strongly lighted than the side of the subject toward the Kodak. Various schemes can be figured out to get such a background.

SILHOUETTES FOR GREETING CARDS

Clever and distinctively personal greeting cards can be made with photographic silhouettes. If you do not wish to do all of the work just hand the negative of the subject to be used to your photo finisher and he will make up the completed cards for you.

On the preceding pages there are numbers of subject ideas.

There is much virgin territory in the land of silhouette making and we have only indicated, in a small way, its possibilities. Once you start on this fascinating phase of photography many novel ideas will present themselves.

Outdoor silhouettes are easy against the sky when the sun is obscured by a cloud. This one, 1/100 second, stop f.22.

LEFT: *Balls are cardboard discs, stuck to sheet.*

Travel subjects for silhouettes.

Water makes a good background.

A cardboard parrot.

A panel of silhouettes makes a good decoration for a child's room.

PHOTOGRAPHIC
CAMEOS

THESE interesting and unique bas-relief effects are easy to obtain from ordinary negatives in which the images are boldly outlined.

The procedure is this.

Make a film positive, that is, a print on film, from the negative, then place this positive over the negative and make a print.

The result obtained will depend on how nearly the density of the positive equals the density of the negative and on how much out of register the positive is with the negative.

When a positive that is of the same density throughout as the negative is placed over the negative, so that all parts of the positive image are in perfect register with all parts of the negative image, the positive will neutralize the negative so that no image can be seen by looking through the films. This is the ideal combination for making photographic cameos, which can be obtained from two such films by merely moving the positive so it will be slightly out of register with the negative and then making a print in the usual way.

The effect can be varied by the amount of shifting of the positive and by its density.

Suitable positives can be made on Kodak Roll Film, Kodak Film Pack Film and Kodak Cut Film. Those who have darkrooms that are light-proof can use the same film for making the positives that they use for making negatives, but as negative film is extremely sensitive to light, care must be taken not to overprint the positive.

When using ordinary negative film place a sheet of ground glass over the front of the printing frame for diffusing and subduing the light, and print the positive by the light of a small pocket flashlamp, or by the light of a match, either of which should be held about eighteen inches from the center of the printing frame. No definite rule can be given for the length of time to print, but the exposure to either of the lights mentioned, will be very brief, usually from 2 to 5 seconds, depending on the speed of the film.

Those who have no photographic darkroom will find it a very simple matter to make positives on Eastman Commercial Cut Film, which, with care, can be manipulated in any darkened room at night. With a negative of normal density sufficient exposure will be obtained by switching a 25-watt Mazda lamp on and off as quickly as possible with the printing frame held thirty inches from the light.

Eastman Commercial Film is too sensitive for developing by any light that is strong enough to read by, but it can be safely developed in a bright red light, which is obtained when a Wratten Series 2 Safelight is used in a Kodak or a Brownie Safelight Lamp.

Positives of different densities can be secured by developing films that

The best "cameos" are made from negatives with good contrasts.

169

received the same exposure for different lengths of time. The positives made should record all the detail that is in the negative.

The illustrations on pages 168 and 169 show but two of the many interesting effects that can be obtained by the method described. This method is as suitable for making enlargements as it is for making contact prints. When several pictures are to be made from the same negative and positive, it is best to fasten one edge of the films together with gummed paper, so the register will not be shifted while the films are in the frame.

Photographic cameos that are surrounded by white margins are especially pleasing. The easiest way to mask the films for securing white margin prints is by using the Kodak Auto-Mask Printing Frame described on page 217.

THE RINK AT ROCKEFELLER CENTER, NEW YORK—*As illustrated here, the "shot" made from an unusual angle frequently produces a better picture than if taken in the ordinary way.*

Yet the photographer was lucky on several points: it is difficult to imagine how the figures of the skaters and of the groups of spectators could have been allocated to better advantage. The late afternoon sun aided by casting long shadows from skaters, dividing the rink diagonally, and by keeping all save the "stage" in a sufficiently low key.

170 *Made with Kodak Duo Six-20 on "SS" Pan Film, 1/200 second at f.6.3.*

PICTURE-MAKING THROUGH A
MICROSCOPE

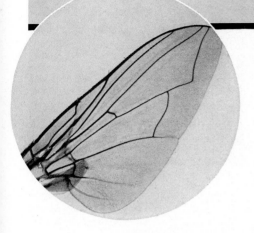

The wing of a common house fly; 20x magnification.

PHOTOMICROGRAPHY is a most fascinating branch of photography for everyone and is, of course, of great value to the student of biology and natural history. Too, it is a phase of picture making that provides interesting subjects the year around.

Possessing a microscope (it need not be an expensive one) and any camera, even one of the box type, with a "time" adjustment, you can assemble a satisfactory photomicrographic outfit by constructing a stand to hold the camera firmly in position to the eye piece of the microscope.

USING ORDINARY CAMERAS

While a camera designed for cut film and having a ground-glass focusing screen, like the Kodak Recomar, is more readily adapted for this work, any camera equipped to take time exposures may be used. With folding cameras that have no ground glass upon which to focus an image, a thin piece may be placed over the opening at the back. The ground side of the glass should face the camera lens. Where it is not practicable to do this, so that focusing may be done visually, the lens should be set at the 100-foot mark. A camera without a lens may be used but in such a case focusing must be done on the ground glass.

In addition to a firm support which will permit the camera to be raised or lowered, a light-tight connection between microscope and camera is essential. This may be a piece of black velvet, or similar

A sugar crystal, 50 x magnification.

material that will not let light through, wound loosely around the proper parts of the apparatus.

The next step is to place the subject in a position on the "stage" of the microscope and adjust the light source and mirror so that the field is properly illuminated. Then focus the image sharply through the microscope. Now bring the camera down into position over the microscope and make the light-tight connection. All being in readiness, the exposure can now be made in the usual manner, taking great care not to jar the camera or microscope.

ILLUMINATION AND EXPOSURE

As daylight varies considerably from hour to hour, it is a bit difficult, at least for the novice, to determine the proper daylight exposure. For this reason it is better to use electric light. A 40- or 50-watt frosted bulb in an ordinary goose-neck desk lamp will serve excellently.

Modern films have emulsions with such wide latitude that exposure timings need

A silk stocking, 50 x magnification.

not be exact but may be varied within reasonable limits and still produce a satisfactory picture. It is difficult to recommend any precise figures for exposure because of the wide choice of subjects, the magnification desired, kind of film used, and other varying conditions under which the pictures may be made. However, an exposure of somewhere from one to five seconds will usually produce satisfactory results. This will at least give an idea for a start. It would be well to make a series of test exposures by taking one picture at an estimated exposure, then two others, one with six times less exposure and another with six times longer exposure. After a few trials, it becomes possible to estimate exposures with sufficient accuracy. It should be remembered that as magnification increases, exposure must also increase.

The use of a filter will often produce much better results in cases where the subject is distinctly colored. The exposure time must, of course, be lengthened as called for by the filter factor. Information regarding the choice and use of the proper filter is contained in the book, "Photomicrography," which may be purchased through your Kodak dealer.

THE FILM TO USE

For the beginner any medium-speed, color-sensitive (orthochromatic) film may be used. Verichrome, which is highly orthochromatic, will yield quite satisfactory pictures. For best results with stained slides, use a panchromatic negative material and suitable filter. Kodak Panatomic Film is ideal.

173

The lighting of this chess study has been cleverly handled.

IF YOU WANT TO DO YOUR OWN

Roll film developing with the Kodak Film Tank requires no darkroom.

DEVELOPING
PRINTING
ENLARGING
COLORING

Excellent finishing of pictures is being done by photo finishers who give prompt service from conveniently located stores. Some photography enthusiasts prefer, however, to "follow through" after having clicked off a series of exposures.

To them the various steps of creating a finished picture, from the invisible or "latent" image on the film, are intensely fascinating. It all smacks somewhat of magic.

TANK METHOD

This method of developing roll film may be done in subdued daylight with the Kodak Film Tank which, in effect, is its own darkroom. With this system, no technical knowledge is re-

Making the prints is a fascinating pastime.

The Kodak Film Tank

quired — the experience is in the Tank. Development is done wholly by time and temperature, which are fixed quantities. This is the method employed by the commercial photo finisher in handling the large quantities of film he receives every day.

By means of the light-tight box the film is transferred to a reel, being covered at the same time by a protecting apron. Reel, film, and apron are then immersed in the solution cup, and development is completed according to directions that accompany the Tank.

The Kodak Film Tank lends itself ideally to the development of Super X Pan, "SS" Pan and Panatomic Films. Because of the extreme sensitivity of these materials, they must, after exposure, be handled in total darkness. The ingenious construction and method of operation of this tank and of the new Kodak Adjustable Film Tank make them the safest and surest devices for the amateur's use.

THE KODAK ADJUSTABLE ROLL FILM TANK

This tank is very convenient for developing roll films of all the popular sizes, from widths of 35 mm. to 2½ inches. The film is wound onto a reel in a darkroom. The reel with the film is then lowered into the tank containing the developer and the light-tight cover is placed on the tank.

Developing and all the other operations for processing the film; rinsing, fixing and washing are done in the tank in the ordinary light of the room; no trays are necessary. The various solutions are rapidly changed through an opening in the light-tight cover.

The Kodak Adjustable Roll Film Tank assures uniform development.

175

Parts of the Kodak Adjustable Roll Film Tank.

After the film is wound onto the reel it is not touched until it is removed and hung up to dry; thus avoiding the possibility of scratches or finger marks. There is a choice of four developers for processing the film. A similar tank is available for pack film and cut film. See page 183. A unit, from this tank, is available to owners of the Kodak Adjustable Roll Film Tank who wish to adapt it for pack film and cut film developing. For cut film developing the Kodak Developing Box, No. 1 is also available. See page 189. Full instructions accompany each tank.

The stainless steel tank holds 32 ounces of developer.

While tank development offers greater convenience and protects the novice from his own inexperience many experts also prefer it. With roll film, in the Kodak Film Tank, it is daylight all the way. With the Kodak Adjustable Film Tanks all operations, except loading, are carried on in ordinary room light as mentioned.

DEVELOPER FOR TANK DEVELOPMENT

The Kodak Tank Developer Powders are Pyro developer powders pre-

*The G filter helps to deepen shadow rendering in
snow scenes and aids in recording distant objects.*

pared especially for use with the tank. If you wish to prepare your own developer follow the formula given for your particular tank. Formulas are on the following pages.

Develop the film for the length of time as given in the table according to the temperature of the developer. (See table on page 179.)

Temperature of the developer should not exceed 70° F. (21° C.). The time of development should be reduced one minute for each degree rise of temperature assuming 15 minutes' development at 70° F. (21° C.) as in the table on page 179. When the temperature of the solution is greater than 70° F. (21° C.) it is not possible to use the Kodak Film Tank and a special processing technic is necessary as described in the booklet "Tropical Development," obtainable on request from the Service Department, Eastman Kodak Company, Rochester, N. Y.

It is not advisable to use water that is colder than 55° F. (12.5° C.) as below this temperature the chemicals dissolve too slowly and the time of development is too long, and even at this temperature the powder must be finely crushed and added slowly to the water.

TIME AND TEMPERATURE — TANK SYSTEM

After the developer has been properly prepared, *test the temperature with a thermometer.* Best results are obtained when the temperature of the developer is 65° F. (18° C.).

If, however, the temperature of the developer is exactly 70° F. (21° C.)

"WATERFRONT"

To some this technically good picture may seem too "busy"; too many horizontal, vertical and curving lines. To others the effect may be interesting. This is one of those subjects which call for study after the first cursory glance.

Vistas are always intriguing and give a feeling of stereoscopic or third-dimensional effect. Lighting, too, plays a major role. Train your eye to "see" such pictures; then shoot them from various angles and choose the best.

Taken with a Kodak Duo Six-20 on Panatomic Film, 1/25 second at f.11 with K2 filter.

develop the film fifteen minutes, then for every degree colder than 70 degrees, add one minute to the time for development. For example: if the developer is 65 degrees, develop the film 20 minutes; if 62 degrees, develop 23 minutes, etc. as indicated in the table below.

Table of Time and Temperature for Tank Development for Regular, Verichrome, "SS" Panchromatic, and Panatomic Films

Temperature Fahr.	Time (One Pair of Powders)	Temperature Fahr.	Time (One Pair of Powders)
70 Degrees (21° C.)	15 Minutes	62 Degrees............	23 Minutes
69 "	16 "	61 "	24 "
68 "	17 "	60 " (15° C.)	25 "
67 "	18 "	59 "	26 "
66 "	19 "	58 "	27 "
65* " (18° C.)	20 "	57 "	28 "
64 "	21 "	56 "	29 "
63 "	22 "	55 " (12.5° C) ...	30 "

*Recommended

Developer Formulas

2¼-INCH KODAK FILM TANK

	Avoirdupois	Metric
Sodium Sulphite, desiccated (E.K.Co.)....	20 grains	1.4 grams
Sodium Carbonate, desiccated (E.K.Co.)..	25 grains	1.7 grams
Pyro.................................	10 grains	0.7 gram
Water, to fill cup to embossed ring.		

2½- AND 3½-INCH KODAK FILM TANKS

Sodium Sulphite, desiccated (E.K.Co.)....	44 grains	3.0 grams
Sodium Carbonate, desiccated (E.K.Co.)..	55 grains	3.8 grams
Pyro.................................	22 grains	1.5 grams
Water, to fill cup to embossed ring.		

Dissolve the chemicals in the order given above.

Temperature of Developer should be between 60 and 70 degrees F.

The colored backing on films may not be entirely removed from places where the film was in contact with the paper, thus giving a blotchy appearance when first separated from the apron. This effect usually disappears in the fixing bath, but if a slight stain remains, it will do no harm. It can, however, be removed by

placing the negative in a weak solution of sodium sulphite, made by dissolving
20 grains of sulphite (des.) in a pint of clear water.

SHORT DEVELOPMENT

If it is desired to shorten the time of development good results may be obtained by
using two pairs of powders or doubling all
the quantities of chemicals in the formulas
and developing for half the time given in
the table on page 179.

If an Elon-Hydroquinone non-staining
developer is desired use the Eastman Film
and Plate Developer Tube, page 165. One
tube of developer will make 32 ounces of
solution. Make up the developer and add

Fixing a strip of negatives.

enough of the solution to the cup to fill it to the embossed ring.
Develop the film about twelve minutes at 65° F. (18° C.).

FINE GRAIN DEVELOPMENT

For negatives of finest grain, permitting of extreme enlargement, the
new Eastman Ultra-Fine-Grain Developer is recommended. This is
a non-staining developer for rapid development of "SS" Pan, Super X
Pan, Panatomic, and other films. It is supplied in quantities that make
up a pint or a quart of solution, ready to use. For maximum shadow
detail, the negative should be given twice normal exposure.

THE FIXING BATH

Provide a box of Kodak Acid Fixing Powders for the fixing bath, and
prepare according to the instructions on the package. The temperature
of the fixing bath should not exceed 70° F. (21° C.).

The fixing bath may be prepared without a graduate. The
average tumbler holds approximately eight ounces; you can, therefore,
get your fixing bath near enough to the right strength by its use.

Pass the film face down (the face, after development, is the side on
which the image appears clearly) through the fixing solution as shown
in the illustration, holding one end in each hand. Do this three or four
times and then place one end of the film in the tray (8 x 10 inches is a

good size), still face down, and lower the strip into the solution in folds. Gently press the film where the fold occurs, not tightly enough to crease it, down into the solution a few times during the course of fixing. This insures the fixing solution reaching every part of the film. Allow the film to remain about twenty minutes or for twice the time necessary to clear it of the milky appearance. Then remove for washing.

If preferred, negatives may be cut apart and fixed separately.

Kodak Film should always be fixed in an acid bath. Kodak Acid Fixing Powders or the following formula may be used.

ACID HARDENING FIXING BATH (*Formula F-5*)

For Films and Plates

		Avoirdupois		Metric
Water (about 125° F.) (52° C.)	32	ounces		1.0 liter
Hypo	16	ounces		480.0 grams
Sodium Sulphite, desiccated (E.K.Co.)	1	ounce		30.0 grams
*Acetic Acid, 28% pure (E. K. Co.)	3	fluid ozs.		96.0 c.c.
**Boric Acid, crystals	½	ounce		15.0 grams
Potassium Alum (E.K.Co.)	1	ounce		30.0 grams
Water to make	64	ounces		2.0 liters

*To make 28% acetic acid from glacial acetic acid dilute three parts of glacial acid with eight parts of water.

**Use crystalline boric acid as specified. Powdered boric acid is difficult to dissolve and its use should be avoided.

Dissolve the chemicals in the order given.

This bath may be made up at any time in advance and be used so long as it will fix films in twenty minutes and is not sufficiently discolored by developer carried into it to stain the negatives. The temperature of the bath should not be over 70° F. (21° C.).

181

A properly fixed and thoroughly washed print will keep indefinitely.

WASHING

All negatives must be washed thoroughly so as to remove every trace of hypo and other foreign substance. Where running water is accessible the films may be placed in a tray or washing box and left under a faucet from which runs a gentle stream, for about 30 minutes. The flow of water should be such that the water is replaced completely in the tray once every five minutes. Films should be moved from time to time, so that the washing may be thorough and complete. Do not crowd too many films in too small a tray during the process. Where running water is not accessible the negatives may be placed in a tray or bowl of cold water, and left to soak for five minutes, when the water should be changed and the process repeated eight times. The temperature of the wash water should not exceed 70° F. (21° C.), otherwise the gelatin coating of the film will tend to soften.

DRYING FILM NEGATIVES

The Improved Kodak Film Clip for drying negatives.

When thoroughly washed, wipe the surface of the film carefully with a soft sponge or chamois to remove all excess drops of water. Then snap a Kodak or Kodak Jr. Film Clip on each end of the strip and hang it up to dry or pin it up. Be sure, however, that it swings clear of the wall so that there will be no possibility of either side of the film coming in contact with the wall or any other object, and do not have the film where the direct sunlight will strike it.

If the film has been cut apart, pin each negative, by one corner, to the edge of a shelf or hang them on a stretched string by means of a bent pin, running the pin through the corner of the film to the head, then hooking it over the string.

182

Good pictures like this can be spoiled very easily by careless finishing.

DEVELOPING PACK FILM AND CUT FILM

THERE are two Eastman tanks for pack film: the Kodak Adjustable Cut Film and Film Pack Tank, and the Kodak Film Pack Tank.

The adjustable tank takes either pack or cut film in all amateur sizes from 4.5x6 cm. to 3¼x4¼ inches. With this tank developing, fixing and washing are car-

The Kodak Adjustable Cut Film and Film Pack Tank

ried on in the tank itself. It is only necessary that loading be done in the dark. Any closet, made totally dark, and with room enough for a small table, will serve. Complete directions are furnished with each tank. To convert this tank for roll film, simply procure a Kodak Adjustable Roll Film Developing Reel Unit.

DEVELOPER FOR ADJUSTABLE TANK

The following developers are recommended: Eastman Universal Developer Powders, Eastman Film and Plate Developer Powders, Eastman Prepared D-76 Developer Powders, or Eastman Ultra-Fine-Grain Developer Powders. When prepared, the Eastman D-76 Developer and the Eastman Ultra-Fine-Grain Developer can be kept for about six months in filled, tightly corked bottles.

FIXING BATH

Obtain a ½-pound package of Kodak Acid Fixing Powder and prepare it according to the directions on the carton.

The Kodak Film Pack Tank

THE KODAK FILM PACK TANK

This is an inexpensive outfit for pack films only. Exposed films are bent double and slid into separate compartments of the metal cage. The loaded cage is then lowered into the tank. Fixing should not be carried on in this tank. Loading must be done in the dark.

DEVELOPER FOR FILM PACK TANK

Developer powders for these tanks are put up in packages of one-half dozen pairs. Eastman Film and Plate Developer may be used and also the Ultra-Fine-Grain Developer (page 197).

Formulas follow for those who wish to mix their own developer.

FORMULAS FOR KODAK FILM PACK TANK

FOR NO. 1 KODAK FILM PACK TANK:

	Avoirdupois	Metric
Sodium Sulphite, desiccated (E.K.Co.)	60 grains	4.2 grams
Sodium Carbonate, desiccated (E.K.Co.)	75 grains	5.2 grams
Pyro	22 grains	1.5 grams

Water, to fill cup to embossed ring.

FOR NO. 2 KODAK FILM PACK TANK:

Sodium Sulphite, desiccated (E.K.Co.)	120 grains	8.4 grams
Sodium Carbonate, desiccated (E.K.Co.)	150 grains	10.3 grams
Pyro	45 grains	3.1 grams

Water, to fill cup to embossed ring.

Dissolve the chemicals in the order given; first the sulphite in four or five ounces of water, then add the carbonate and finally the Pyro, and fill the tank to the embossed ring with cold water.

For temperature and time follow the table on page 179.

FIXING

For fixing see directions and formula on pages 180 and 181.

DEVELOPING PACK FILM BY THE DARKROOM METHOD

After removing the exposed films from the pack the black protecting papers to which they will be found attached should be removed and each film placed emulsion side down in a tray of water. (The emulsion side, or face, is the dull side.) They should be allowed to stand two or three minutes and then each film should be placed separately in the developing tray, still face down. The tray should be rocked gently from time to time, the films never being allowed to mat together, and the progress of development ascertained by holding the film up to the light of the

The Kodak Darkroom Outfit No. 1.

lamp. Verichrome and Kodak Film (Regular) in pack form must be developed 20% longer than roll film if other than the developer for the tank is used. Panatomic and "SS" Pan should be developed for the same time as the corresponding roll film.

After completing development transfer to fixing bath. See pages 180 and 181. Then wash and dry as described on page 182.

DETAILS OF DARKROOM DEVELOPMENT

Of the two methods of developing, darkroom, with trays, or the day-light tank, the former is perhaps the more interesting. With it a darkroom, lighted only by a photographically safe light, is required and, in addition, there must of course be the trays for the solutions, and running water, at least nearby. A corner of the basement, a big closet, an attic room—any place that can be made totally dark can be fitted up for tray developing. In this kind of developing you can watch the latent image gradually build up on the apparently blank film. With this method a little experience will soon enable the beginner to produce good results.

The Kodak Darkroom Outfit No. 1, pictured here, is well suited to the requirements of beginner or advanced worker, and can also be used as a basis for permanent darkroom equipment by camera clubs.

This outfit includes a Brownie Safelight Lamp (with Series 2 Safe-light, unless otherwise specified), 10-watt Mazda Bulb, Kodak Auto-Mask Printing Frame, two 4 x 6 Enameled Trays, 5 x 7 Enameled Tray,

185

8-ounce Eastko Graduate, Hard Rubber Stirring Rod, Eastman Thermometer, two Kodak Junior Film Clips, 6 blotters (size 9½ x 12 inches), 1 package Eastman M. Q. Developer, 1 package Eastman Film and Plate Developer, 1 pound Kodak Acid Fixing Powder, instruction booklet, and a copy of "How to Make Good Pictures" which makes an ideal gift to a "photographic" friend if you already own a copy. Kodak dealers have this and other outfits from which you can make a choice.

THE DARKROOM

The first essential is the darkroom. By a darkroom is meant one that has been made *entirely* dark—not a ray of white light entering it. Such a room can easily be secured at night almost anywhere. A comfortable working light can be used if it comes from a safelight lamp. The reason a totally dark room is required is that the film is extremely sensitive to *white* light, either daylight or electric light, *and would be spoiled if exposed to a ray of it* even for a fraction of a second.

If possible have running water but if this is not available provide a container for water, a shelf or table on which to work, and a pair of shears.

Also obtain a developing outfit such as described on these pages.

Having provided a room or closet, where, when the door is closed, no ray of white light can be seen, set upon the table or shelf the safelight lamp. The Kodak Safelight Lamp illustrated here, or the Brownie Safelight Lamp, shown in use on page 187, or the Brownie Darkroom Lamp, which also screws into a light socket, offers most satisfactory and safe illumination, each giving a subdued red light of the proper hue which will not injure ordinary film or Verichrome Film unless held too close to it or for too long a time. See special directions on page 188, for developing "SS" Pan, Panatomic, or any panchromatic negative material by using Series 3—dark green— Wratten Safelight.

Kodak Safelight Lamp. Ideal for the beginner or advanced worker.

PREPARATIONS

1. Set the lamp on the table at least eighteen inches from the developing

tray an fill one of the trays nearly full of water (first tray).

2. Open one of the developer powders; thoroughly dissolve the contents of one compartment of the packet in a little water; then add water and dissolve second powder. Stir until dissolved, dilute to the volume called for in the instructions, and pour into second tray.

3. To develop, unroll film and detach entire strip from paper.

There is fascination in developing.

4. Pass the film *face down* (the face is the dull side) through the tray of clean water (65° F.) (18° C.), holding one end in each hand. Pass through the water several times, that there may be no bubbles remaining on the film. When thoroughly wet, with no air bubbles, it is ready for development.

5. Now pass the film still *face down* through the developer in the same manner as described for wetting it. Keep it constantly in motion, and in about one minute the highlights will begin to darken and you will readily be able to distinguish the unexposed sections between the negatives, and in about two minutes will be able to distinguish objects in the pictures. Complete development of the strip, giving sufficient time for developer to bring out all possible detail in the thinnest negatives. There is no harm in having your negatives of different densities. This can be taken care of in the printing on Velox paper.

Be sure to keep the strip which is being developed in motion, allowing the developer to act for 5 to 6 minutes. The progress may be watched by holding the negatives up to the lamp from time to time.

When developing regular Kodak Film, use a Kodak or Brownie Safelight Lamp, or a Brownie Darkroom Lamp, taking care not to hold the film close to the lamp for more than four or five seconds at a time.

The extra speed of Verichrome Film has made it necessary to use a deeper red light than formerly in darkroom developing.

The Series 2 Wratten Safelight used with a ten-watt bulb in a Brownie or Kodak Safelight Lamp should be safe for as long as five minutes at a distance of six feet, two minutes at three feet, one minute at one and one-half feet.

Panchromatic Negative Materials:

The color sensitivity of Panatomic, "SS" Pan and other panchromatic films makes it necessary to develop in total darkness. No light of any kind can be used in preparing film or during the first three minutes in developer.

After the film has been in the developer for not less than three minutes, it may be inspected for a brief interval, if a Series 3 (dark green) Wratten Safelight is used in a darkroom fitted with a 10-watt bulb. This lamp must be six feet or more from the film.

Examine your darkroom before developing and see that all white light, causing fog, is excluded. Fog is also often caused by the negative being exposed to white light after development, but before fixing, and if the negative is exposed to light before the developing solution has been washed out, a reversal of the image will frequently be found.

After completing development, transfer to the third tray and rinse two or three times with clean, cold water, and transfer at once to fixing bath. (Page 181.) Then wash and dry as described on page 150.

Elon-Hydroquinone-Borax Developer (*Formula D-76*)

For use with Panatomic and other Panchromatic Films

		Avoirdupois	Metric
Water (about 125° F.) (52° C.)......		24 ounces	750.0 c.c.
Elon.............................		29 grains	2.0 grams
Sodium Sulphite desiccated (E.K.Co.)	3 ozs.	145 grains	100.0 grams
Hydroquinone...................		73 grains	5.0 grams
Borax, granular (E. K. Co.)........		29 grains	2.0 grams
Cold water to make..............		32 ounces	1.0 liter

Dissolve chemicals in the order named. Use without dilution.

Develop Panatomic and "SS" Panchromatic roll film and film packs about 16 minutes at 65° F. (18° C.) in a tray, or 20 minutes in a tank of fresh developer.

A faster working developer may be obtained by increasing the quantity of borax. By increasing the borax to 290 grains for each 32 ounces

188

of developer (20 grams per liter) the development time will be about one-half that required with regular D-76. Maximum activity can be obtained by substituting Kodalk for borax and using 290 grains per 32 ounces of developer (20 grams per liter). With this concentration the contrast of a negative developed for 5 minutes in the more rapid developer will approximate that obtained in 20 minutes in D-76.

Greater or less contrast may be obtained by developing longer or shorter times than those specified.

DEVELOPING CUT FILM IN THE KODAK DEVELOPING BOX NO. 1

THE corrosion resisting, seamless, heavy metal Kodak Developing Box No. 1 is for developing, fixing and washing cut film 3½ x 5½, 4 x 5 and smaller. For suspending the film in the box secure Kodak Cut Film Developing Hangers.

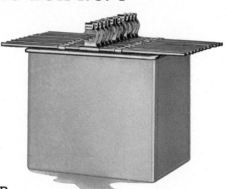

PREPARING THE DEVELOPER

The developer that is recommended for use in the Kodak Developing Box No. 1 is the regular 5 x 7 Eastman Plate Tank Developer Powders. The developer is prepared in the following manner: Fill the box with 64 ounces of water. Test the temperature of the water with a thermometer and bring it to 65° F. (18°C.). Place an empty film hanger in position across the box and if the water does not touch the clips, add water until it comes a little above the bottom of the clips. This is to make sure that the films are entirely covered.

Pour out from four to eight ounces of the water in the box, into a graduate or glass and dissolve in it the contents of the red package. When this powder is dissolved, then add the contents of the blue package. After this is dissolved, pour it back into the box and stir the

189

solution thoroughly. The developer is now ready for use. If some of the contents of the blue package sticks to the paper dip the paper into the solution so that all the contents will be added to the developer.

The developer must always be mixed *fresh* and *used but once*.

The Eastman Film and Plate Developer can also be used in this box. Two tubes, each dissolved in 32 ounces of water, will be necessary to fill the box. This developer may be saved and used several times over a period of one month after mixing. For negatives of finest grain use Eastman Ultra-Fine-Grain Developer. Two quart size cans of the developer are required to make up the necessary volume of solution (see page 197).

DEVELOPER FORMULA

If you wish to prepare your own developer, use the following formula:

Pyro-Soda Developer (*Formula D-70*)

	Avoirdupois	Metric
Water.	32 ounces	1.0 liter
Sodium Sulphite, desiccated (E.K.Co.).	110 grains	7.7 grams
Sodium Bisulphite (E.K.Co.).	10 grains	0.7 gram
Pyro.	60 grains	4.2 grams
Sodium Carbonate, desiccated (E.K.Co.).	80 grains	5.6 grams
Potassium Bromide.	6 grains	0.4 gram
Water to make.	64 ounces	2.0 liters

Dissolve the chemicals in the order given.

Temperature of Developer must be 65° F. (18° C.).
Time of Development about fifteen minutes.

PLACING FILM IN HANGERS

As the exposed films are sensitive to white light, they must be loaded into the film hangers and placed in the developing box in the darkroom.

Take a film hanger in the left hand and centering the film (see page 191), insert the edge (on the long side of film) in the jaws of one of the clips, then press firmly on the lower part of the clip so that film is held securely; now attach the other clip in the same manner.

Caution: When handling the exposed films do not place the fingers on the emulsion or dull side of the film, but hold it by the lower edge.

After the film has been fastened in both clips, take hold of the bottom edge of film and pull it, to see whether the film is clasped tightly by the clips. If the film is not securely fastened and comes loose from the hanger, it will fall to bottom of box and the negative will be ruined.

Load all the films into the hangers before putting them in the developer and place them on a clean sheet of paper that is free from dust, keeping the films apart in order to avoid all danger of scratching them.

DEVELOPING

Put each film in the developing box *separately*, in rapid succession, placing hangers so that the rods rest on the edges of the short sides of box (see page 189), taking care that none of the films come in contact with the sides of the box or with each other. Twelve films or less can be developed at one time. Develop but one size of film at a time. If different sizes are developed at the same time, it will cause uneven develop-

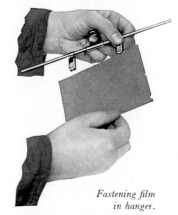

*Fastening film
in hanger.*

ment and streaked negatives. Keep the hangers separated.

If several films are placed in the box simultaneously they will stick together, causing development streaks, which will remain even though films are separated immediately after immersion in box.

Raise the hangers about one-half inch, one at a time, and tap them sharply several times on the side of the tank. After developing one minute lift each hanger out of the solution and immerse again. Then allow development to go to completion. When development has been finished pour out the developer and fill the box with clear cold water leaving the films in the water for about one minute, then pour out the water. Repeat this rinsing three times in order to eliminate all developer from the films, then pour in the previously prepared fixing bath.

SHORT DEVELOPMENT

If it is desired to shorten the length of time for development, two pairs of the powders, or double the quantity of the chemicals as given in the formula may be used. If this is done, the time for development must be one-half the time that is given for development when the regular strength developer is used.

FIXING

The fixing bath should be prepared in a separate container before starting the development of the films, following the procedure described on page 181.

Make sure that the bath entirely covers the films; add more water, if necessary, to bring the level of the solution to the bottom of the clips. Raise the films several times during the fixing, in order that they may be evenly fixed. Allow the films to remain in the solution four or five minutes after the milky appearance has disappeared from them; this will require about twenty minutes.

CAUTION: The Kodak Developing Box No. 1 must not be used as a storage tank for an acid fixing bath. The bath should not be allowed to remain in it longer than is needed for fixing films; the box and hangers must be *thoroughly* washed after using for this purpose.

WASHING

After pouring off the fixing solution allow the films to remain in the developing box, and place the box under a tap of running cold water. Attach a rubber tube to the faucet, long enough to carry the water to bottom of box. This insures complete circulation of water. Leave the films washing for half an hour in this manner, with the rate of flow adjusted so that the water in the tank is replaced once every five minutes. If running water is not available, fill the developing box with cold water and allow the films to remain for five minutes each in eight changes of water. Move the films about occasionally, so that they may be thoroughly and evenly washed. The temperature of the wash water should not exceed 70° F. (21° C.).

DRYING

When washing is complete wipe the film surfaces carefully with a fine soft sponge or chamois to remove excess drops of water before drying. Then hang the negatives by means of the hook on the Developing Hangers, on a stretched string or wire. Negatives should be dried quickly and where there is a continuous draft of air. Slow drying in a warm, close atmosphere has a tendency to destroy even gradation.

Any sudden or great change in temperature while drying is likely to cause unequal density.

CORRECT TEMPERATURE IS IMPORTANT

This stirring rod is ideal for recording temperatures, mixing

Thermometer Stirring Rod.

ingredients, and to crush lumpy powders. A hard rubber rod is available as is also a curved back metal thermometer for tray or tank use.

Eastman Studio Scales.

IF YOU MIX YOUR OWN

The precise weighing of chemicals is as important as their strength, if formulas are to be compounded with accuracy. The Eastman Studio Scales provide an ideal instrument for all who mix their own chemicals. A graduated beam is scaled for minor weights. Larger quantities are weighed by accurately turned metal pan weights. Furnished in either metric or avoirdupois system.

OVER-DEVELOPMENT

Over-development may be caused by leaving the film in the developer too long, by using the solution too warm, or (by those who mix their own chemicals) getting the developing agent too strong.

In such cases a negative is likely to be blocked-up and dense as seen by transmitted light, and requires a long time to print.

The remedy is to reduce it by using Eastman Reducer, or by the following method:

First soak the negative in water for twenty minutes, then immerse in:

REDUCER (*Formula R-4*)

	Avoirdupois	*Metric*
Solution No. 1		
Potassium Ferricyanide....................	15 grains	1.0 gram
Water to make..........................	1 ounce	32.0 c.c.
Solution No. 2		
Hypo.................................	1 ounce	30.0 grams
Water to make..........................	32 ounces	1.0 liter

Add solution No. 1 to solution No. 2 and immediately pour over the negative to be reduced. This formula should be prepared immediately before using as it decomposes rapidly. When the negative has been reduced sufficiently, wash thoroughly before drying.

LOCAL REDUCTION

Negatives may be reduced locally by applying the foregoing solution to the dense parts with a camel's hair brush, rinsing off the reducer with clean water frequently to prevent it from running onto the parts of the negative that do not require reducing.

Should the reduced negative show any yellowness or stain it may be removed by placing it in an Acid Fixing Bath for a few minutes; then the negative should be thoroughly washed (see page 182).

UNDER-DEVELOPMENT

Under-development is caused by removing films from the developer too soon, by using solutions too cold, or by an error in compounding the formula.

It is obvious that none of these defects will occur if instructions for tank development are properly followed.

The remedy for under-development is to intensify by re-development, or with the following formula and method:

INTENSIFICATION BY RE-DEVELOPMENT

CHROMIUM INTENSIFIER (*Formula In-4*)

Stock Solution

	Avoirdupois	Metric
Potassium Bichromate.....................	3 ounces	90.0 grams
Hydrochloric Acid, C.P. (E. K. Co.).........	2 fluid ozs.	64.0 c.c.
Water to make..........................	32 ounces	1.0 liter

For use, take one part of stock solution to ten parts of water.

Bleach thoroughly at 65° F. (18° C.) in the above solution, then wash five minutes and redevelop (about five minutes) in artificial light or daylight (not direct sunlight) in any quick acting, non-staining developer containing the normal proportion of Bromide such as Nepera Solution 1:4. Then wash thoroughly and dry. The degree of intensification may be controlled by varying the time of redevelopment.

194

Greater intensification can be secured by repeating the process. The Eastman Chromium Intensifier Powders are equally as satisfactory as this formula, and are supplied in prepared form ready to use simply by dissolving in water.

WARNING: Concentrated developers of the borax type containing a high concentration of sulphite are not suitable for re-development since the sulphite tends to dissolve the silver chloride before the developing agents have time to act on it.

PREPARED RE-DEVELOPERS FOR INTENSIFICATION

Velox or Royal Re-developer for Sepia tones on Velox and Bromide prints is also effective and simple for intensifying film negatives.

ORIGINAL   STRONGLY INTENSIFIED   LESS INTENSIFIED

Showing Effect of Intensification.

Velox or Royal Re-developer may be used in exactly the same manner as for producing Sepia Tones on Velox or Bromide papers. (See pages 211 and 239.)

195

Negatives intensified by re-development are built up evenly, without undue contrast and without staining.

The advantage of being able to use the chemicals for two different purposes (Sepia toning prints or intensifying negatives) is obvious, the results in either case being all that could be desired.

In re-developing negatives be sure that they have been thoroughly fixed and washed before re-developing.

HANDLING PLATES

Plates must be handled in the solutions one at a time, as they would scratch each other if a larger number were put into the trays simultaneously. They should also be developed *face up*.

For fixing plates it is best to procure a fixing box, usually arranged with a set of twelve grooves. Each plate is dropped into a groove for fixing, thus eliminating the danger of scratching or overlapping.

Washing

In washing plates be careful that they do not overlap or touch each other, to avoid the chance of the corners scratching the emulsions.

NOTE—Plates should be developed to the same density as film negatives and may be examined (except Panchromatic) while developing, before the darkroom lamp in the same manner.

After the negatives have been washed *thoroughly* they are ready for drying. They should be stood on edge or placed in a drying rack and kept in a cool place until dry. They are then ready for printing.

DEVELOPER TO USE FOR DARKROOM DEVELOPMENT

Eastman Universal Developer Powders
for films, plates, Velox, Bromide, and similar papers

This developer satisfies every demand of the new negative emulsions as well as working ideally with developing-out papers for both contact printing and enlarging. It is only necessary to dissolve the chemicals in the amount of water specified: for films and plates, for tray use, take 8 ounces and develop about 4 minutes at 65° F. (18° C.); for tank, take 32 ounces and develop about 13 minutes at 65° F. (18° C.); 12 ounces for Velox paper and develop 45 seconds at 70° F. (21° C.); 24 ounces for Bromide paper and develop not less than 1½ minutes at 70° F.

Eastman Film and Plate Developer Tubes

A superior Elon-hydroquinone developer for roll film, cut film, film packs and plates. One tube makes 8 ounces for tray develop-

Winter sports await your camera.

ment or 32 ounces for tank. Development times are as follows:

Develop about 4 minutes in a tray at 65°F. (18° C.).
Develop about 13 minutes in a tank at 65° F. (18° C.).

EASTMAN ULTRA-FINE-GRAIN DEVELOPER

A package developer for negatives of finest grain permitting maximum enlargement. Especially recommended for "miniature" negatives.

For Tank: Develop Panatomic, "SS" Pan, Verichrome, and Kodak

Film (Regular) for about 15 minutes and Super X Pan for about 20 minutes at 65° F. (21° C.).

Greater or less contrast may be obtained by developing for a longer or shorter time than indicated.

For Tray: Develop 20% less than for tank. Develop Kodak (Regular) and Verichrome packs 20% longer than for the corresponding roll film.

For maximum detail film should be given twice normal exposure.

Early morning or late afternoon gives opportunity for pleasingly back-lighted pictures.

197

PRINTING

HAVING developed the negatives the final step in picture making is now in order—making the prints.

The process is simple, but like all others it requires some skill and judgment, both of which can easily be acquired by strict adherence to the given rules and formulas.

Velox, which is identified by the name lightly printed on the back, is the ideal paper for the every-day picture taker and is suitable for every class of work, as is quite evident from the information given on these pages concerning it. Velox should not be confused with Bromide or any other paper; it has distinctive qualities of its own which have never been successfully imitated. Many improvements have recently been made in its manufacture and today Velox is the product of years of experiment.

Velox can be printed by either artificial light or daylight. Like an exposure on film the image is not visible until development is performed.

The two surfaces of Velox, the different grades and degrees of contrast in which it is manufactured, enable the user to produce good prints from almost any type of negative, suiting his tastes as well as the peculiar requirements of the negatives.

SURFACES AND DEGREES OF CONTRAST

Velox is made in two surfaces divided broadly into six degrees of contrast. Choose the surface that you prefer and the degree of contrast best adapted to each negative, following the rule as given under the heading of "The Paper To Use" on page 201.

IDENTIFICATION LABEL

The different degrees of contrast of Velox paper are designated by number and color of band, as follows:

No. 0, package labels marked with a GRAY band.
No. 1, package labels marked with a RED band.
No. 2, package labels marked with a GREEN band.
No. 3, package labels marked with a YELLOW band.
No. 4, package labels marked with a BLUE band.
No. 5, package labels marked with a BROWN band.

Contrast No. 0 is for negatives of excessive contrast.

Contrast No. 1 to be used when printing negatives of extreme contrast, or when soft effects are desired.

Contrast No. 2 is for average or normal negatives, that have good contrast between highlights and shadows (dark and light parts).

Contrast No. 3 is for weak, thin and "flat" negatives that have little contrast.

Contrast No. 4 is for extremely flat, and very thin, weak negatives, also when much contrast is desired in the print.

Contrast No. 5 is for excessively flat negatives which may be very thin or very dense, also when much contrast is desired.

GRADE	SURFACE	DEGREE OF CONTRAST
E	Semi-Matte	0- 1- 2- 3- 4- 5
F	Glossy	0- 1- 2- 3- 4- 5

MANIPULATION

Velox prints may be successfully made, using daylight for exposure. For the beginner we recommend that artificial light be used, as it is much more uniform, and it will, therefore, be easier to obtain satisfactory prints. If daylight is used select a north window, if possible, as the light from this direction will be more uniform.

Choose paper of correct contrast for kind of result desired.

199

Owing to its sensitiveness, the paper should be handled in a very subdued or yellow light, otherwise it will fog. Proper precautions should be taken to pull down the window shades and darken the room sufficiently during manipulation. To test your working light, place an unexposed sheet of the paper you are using, emulsion side up, on your work table in the same position that your developing tray occupies; cover one-half of it with a sheet of cardboard and let it remain there for two minutes, then develop it face down for 45 seconds. If the half of the sheet which was uncovered turns gray, or black, and the covered portion remains white, it is a positive indication that the light you were using is too strong. If, however, the entire sheet remains white, your light is safe. Never handle Velox in a light that will not stand this test. If using daylight and the light is too strong for printing it should be subdued or diffused by the use of several thicknesses of white tissue paper or one thickness of orange or post office paper. In the following instructions for manipulating Velox, it must be understood that artificial light will be the light used. A kerosene lamp, fitted with a round burner (known as a Rochester burner), may be used, but owing to the decidedly yellow light this gives, a considerably longer exposure will be necessary than when using an electric lamp.

Comparative exposures when using Contrast No. 2 Velox, with an average or normal negative, and with various sources of light, are as follows:

Distance from Light	60-Watt Lamp	40-Watt Lamp	25-Watt Lamp	Welsbach Burner (Gas)	Average Oil Lamp
8 Inches	4 Seconds	9 Seconds	17 Seconds	21 Seconds	90 Seconds

NOTE—When using Contrast No. 0 or No. 1 Velox make a slightly shorter exposure, and when using Contrast No. 3, No. 4 or No. 5 Velox increase the exposure. A shorter distance between printing light and negative shortens the exposure.

This table is only approximate, as owing to the different lights used and the varying densities of negatives, it is impossible to give an absolute rule. It serves, however, as a guide to enable the beginner to determine the correct exposure. One definite rule to follow is: *Velox of both surfaces and all degrees of contrast must be exposed so that it develops to the correct depth in about forty-five seconds, at 70° F. (21° C.).*

Print from a negative of good contrast on No. 2, Glossy Velox.

THE PAPER TO USE

Contrast No. 0 is for excessively contrasty negatives or to be used when decidedly soft effects are wanted. No. 1 Velox should be used for negatives of considerable contrast or when fairly soft effects are desired. No. 2 is for the normal, correctly exposed negative. No. 3 is for the slightly underexposed or weak negative. No. 4 should be used when printing from flat, and very thin negatives or when quite a bit of contrast is needed. No. 5 is for excessively flat negatives.

To those familiar with Velox paper it is an easy matter to select the degree of contrast which is best suited for the results desired. The novice, however, is guided usually by the advice of others and often is misled into using a wrong degree of contrast, thereby failing to secure the results expected, and he may be inclined to believe that the paper is at fault. It would, therefore, be advisable to keep on hand the six degrees of contrast and when in doubt as to which should be used this can be easily determined by making comparative tests.

When selecting papers remember that No. 4 Velox is best adapted for use with negatives that have little brilliance or contrast, and that No. 5 is for exceptionally flat negatives which may be very thin or very dense. No. 4 and No. 5 are also good for silhouette negatives.

An overexposed and overdeveloped negative (difficult to illustrate) is very flat and dense throughout, necessitating a long exposure. Such a negative is best printed on No. 4 or No. 5 Velox.

PRINTING REQUISITES

The necessities for making Velox prints are few in number and simple in character. Either daylight or artificial light is, of course, essential;

also developing and fixing solutions and water for washing the prints.

The ordinary printing frame is used when making exposures. If you do not have a developing and printing outfit as described on page 185 you will require these things aside from a suitable light and work-room:

3 trays, preferably enameled iron (a full size larger than the prints to be made).

1 printing frame (and glass to fit, unless plates are to be printed).

1 4-oz. graduate.

1 bottle Nepera Solution or a can of D-72 developer powder.

Pkg. Kodak Acid Fixing ⎫ or 1 bottle Velox Liquid Hardener.
Powder. ⎰ 1 lb. Crystal or Granulated Hypo.

1 thermometer ⎰ Eastman Thermometer or
⎱ Eastman Stirring Rod Thermometer.

1 package each of Velox paper of at least three degrees of contrast; No. 0, No. 2, and No. 4 are suggested.

Arrange the three trays on the work table in this order:

Developer (see page 205) 1	Clean Water 2	Towel	Fixing Bath (see page 207) 3

Do not allow the direct rays of light used for printing to strike tray No. 1, which is used for the developer. Place a piece of yellow or orange colored paper between the light and tray No. 1, so as to obtain a sub-dued and safe light. This will prevent the light fogging the paper.

In the center of the spaces diagrammed above we have indicated what each tray should contain when developing Velox. Do not be too sparing of the amount of solutions used, especially of your fixing bath (tray No. 3); if making four or five dozen prints ($3\frac{1}{4}$ x $5\frac{1}{2}$), use a full quart (see formula, page 207); and do not keep it after using, as a fresh bath will give the best results. If a larger number of prints are made, use a stop bath (page 205) in tray No. 2.

Correct temperature is important and for the best results the temperature of the developer, the fixing bath, and the wash water should be 70 degrees F. (21°C.). If the developer exceeds 70 degrees F. (21°C.) the prints are liable to fog and the emulsion soften. If too cold, chemical action is retarded, resulting in flat, weak prints. If the fixing bath is too warm it will not harden the prints properly and it may turn milky, leaving a deposit on prints.

MAKING THE PRINT

The printing frame should now be used. Place the face or sensitized side of the sheet of Velox against the face or dull side of the negative. The paper curls slightly, the sensitive side being concave.

Place the printing frame the correct distance from the artificial light used, holding the frame away from the light a distance slightly more than the diagonal of the negative, and at a right angle to the source of light. A few seconds exposure will be required when printing an average negative on Velox.

Much can be done in the printing of certain types of negatives to obtain different renderings of the photograph. Here are reproductions of two prints from the same negative, which was made at dusk, just as the city's lights had been switched on. Above is shown the daylight effect from printing the negative in the ordinary way, and below we see the same picture printed much deeper, to give a night effect. This subject is unquestionably more striking, and tells the story better, in the rendition given in the print below.

We suggest, before making the first exposure, the cutting of a piece of Velox paper into strips about an inch wide; placing one of them over an important part of the negative, make the exposure, using your best judgment as to the distance from the light and the time of printing. Develop it and if not satisfied try another strip varying the time as indicated by the first result. When the desired effect is secured, you can make any number of prints from the same negative, and if the time of exposure, distance from light as well as the time of developing are the same as for the satisfactory test print, all succeeding prints will be equally good. By comparing other negatives with the one you have tested you will be able to make a fairly accurate estimate of the exposure required for any negative.

To develop, remove the exposed paper from the printing frame and slide it edgewise and face up into the solution (tray No. 1) to quickly and evenly cover it with the developer. Some workers tip the tray slightly so as to insure the print being covered promptly. *Velox of both surfaces and all degrees of contrast should be exposed so as to develop to the proper depth in about forty-five seconds.* As soon as the image has reached the desired depth remove the print from the developer to the second tray and rinse for at least five seconds in clear water, turning the print once or twice, then place it in the acid fixing bath (tray No. 3), *keeping the print moving for a few seconds, the same as was done when rinsing; move prints about occasionally so as to give even and thorough fixing, preventing stains and other troubles.* Leave the prints in this solution until thoroughly fixed; this will take *fifteen minutes.* When fixed remove from fixing bath and wash thoroughly for about one hour in running water, then dry. The flow should be such that the water in the washing tray is replaced completely once every five minutes. If running water is not available, then the prints may be placed in a tray or washbowl of cold water, and left for five minutes each, in twelve changes of water. This is best done by using two trays, transferring the prints, one at a time, from one tray to the other and refilling with fresh water. Move the prints about occasionally to insure the water acting evenly on the surface of the prints, and to make sure that the hypo is entirely eliminated. After drying (see page 209) prints may be trimmed and mounted.

Be systematic in working. Remember that cleanliness is essential in photography. Care should be taken to prevent the hypo in any way getting into the tray containing the developer. Have a clean towel when beginning work and rinse and wipe the hands each time after handling prints in the fixing bath.

NOTES ON PRINT DEVELOPMENT

Velox requires a special developer and should not be used with one made for plate and film development only. Various developing agents are used in the production of Velox prints and are marketed under different trade names. It has been proved, however, that Elon and Hydroquinone in combination yield the very best results on Velox when used in the proportion given in our formula. Owing to the difficulty many have in securing pure chemicals and the trouble and subsequent loss of material to those attempting to compound their own developers, we recommend the use of our liquid developer, Nepera Solution for Velox papers, also if a tube (dry powder) form of developer, which is merely dissolved in a specified amount of water, is desired, we recommend Eastman M. Q. Developer, Eastman Special Developer or the new Eastman Universal Developer. To those who prefer to prepare their own solution, we advise the following formula:

ELON-HYDROQUINONE DEVELOPER

FOR VELOX PAPER (*Formula D-72*)

Stock Solution

	Avoirdupois		Metric
Water (about 125°F.) (52°C.)	16	ounces	500.0 cc.
Elon	45	grains	3.1 grams
Sodium Sulphite, desiccated (E.K.Co.)	1½	ounces	45.0 grams
Hydroquinone	175	grains	12.0 grams
Sodium Carbonate, desiccated (E.K.Co.)	2¼	ounces	67.5 grams
Potassium Bromide	27	grains	1.9 grams
Cold water to make	32	ounces	1.0 liter

For use with Velox paper take stock solution 1 part, water 2 parts. Develop 45 seconds at 70°F. (21°C.). This formula is also recommended for Bromide papers. Instructions for use with Bromide papers are given on page 233.

In summer, if found necessary to cool the developer, do not place ice *in* the solution, as it will dilute it. Place the tray containing developer into one of larger size, with ice around it.

If using Nepera Solution for Velox paper (any surface or degree of contrast) use it diluted as directed on the label.

ACID RINSE BATH

When a large number of prints are to be made, we recommend that they be rinsed for at least five seconds between developing and fixing, in an acid rinse bath, as its action instantly checks development and prevents uneven spots and streaks when the prints are immersed in the fixing bath.

A fresh bath should be mixed each time and then discarded, as the acid in an old bath will become neutralized by the alkali carried over from the developer.

Acid Rinse Bath *(Formula SB-1)*

	Avoirdupois	Metric
Water...............................	32 ounces	1.0 liter
*Acetic Acid (28% pure) (E.K.Co)........	1½ fluid ozs.	48.0 cc.

To make 28% acetic acid from glacial acetic acid dilute three parts of glacial acid with eight parts of water.

FIXING

Hypo may be obtained for use in either a granulated or crystal form. Its purpose is to dissolve the silver salts which have not been acted upon by light. The importance of the chemical is evident, but it is probable that no part or process of photography is more abused than that of correctly preparing a fixing bath and properly fixing prints. To secure permanency, prints *must* be fixed in a fresh acid fixing bath. When hypo is first dissolved in water, the temperature of the solution is ma-

terially reduced. *It is important that the temperature of a fixing bath should not exceed 70 degrees F. (21°C.).* Probably more prints change color from insufficient fixing than lack of washing, so these points should be given attention. Have plenty of solution, and leave the prints in the fixing bath for *fifteen minutes. Always use the acid hardener in the bath as it will overcome the tendency of the fixing bath to cause blisters and stains. Move the prints about for the first few seconds after immersion to stop the action of the developer*

From a Kodak Panatomic Film negative.

at once over the entire surface of the print. Move the prints about occasionally during the time of fixing, to avoid stains and other troubles. This is important as are also thorough fixation and the replacement of the fixing bath when exhausted. Prints should not be fixed in a bath used for films or plates.

KODAK ACID FIXING POWDER

Kodak Acid Fixing Powder is supplied in packages of different sizes, which contain all the chemicals necessary to prepare a correct acid fixing bath. We recommend its use as it is the most convenient and easy to prepare.

Directions for preparation are given on each package.

If the amateur prefers to mix his own use the following:

ACID HARDENING FIXING BATH (*Formula F-1*)

For Paper

	Avoirdupois	Metric
Water	64 ounces	2.0 liters
Hypo	16 ounces	480.0 grams

When the Hypo is *dissolved thoroughly*, add 4 ozs. 128 cc. Velox Liquid Hardener or the following hardening solution:

	Avoirdupois	Metric
Water (about 125° F.) (52°C.)	5 ounces	160.0 cc.
Sodium Sulphite, desiccated (E.K.Co.)	1 ounce	30.0 grams
*Acetic Acid (28% pure) (E.K.Co.)	3 fluid ozs.	96.0 cc.
Potassium Alum (E.K.Co.)	1 ounce	30.0 grams

* To make 28% acetic acid from glacial acetic acid dilute 3 parts of glacial acid with 8 parts of water.

To mix the hardener dissolve the chemicals in the order given above. The sodium sulphite should be dissolved completely before adding the acetic acid. After the sulphite-acid solution has been mixed thoroughly add the potassium alum with constant stirring. Cool the hardener and add it slowly to the cool hypo solution while stirring the latter rapidly. The hypo should be dissolved completely before adding the hardener; otherwise a precipitate of sulphur is liable to form.

This solution will keep in tightly corked bottles. Sixteen ounces will fix one-half gross of $3\frac{1}{4}$ x $5\frac{1}{2}$ prints or their equivalent in other sizes if acid rinse bath (SB-1, page 206) is used, or about thirty-five $3\frac{1}{4}$ x $5\frac{1}{2}$ prints or their equivalent if only a water rinse is used.

NOTES ON WASHING

The finished prints must be entirely free from hypo. To completely remove all traces of hypo, the prints must be washed at least one hour in a tray in which a constant stream of water is running, sufficient to change the water in the tray at least eight to ten times each hour, or if running water is not available they must be washed in 12 *changes* of water, allowing 5 minutes for each change. Prints will not wash if piled in a heap in a tray and the water simply runs in at one end of the tray and out at the other. In some localities where there is an excessive amount of iron or impurity in the water, the whites in the prints may have a slight yellowish tone or small red spots may appear. These can be prevented by filtering the water used through several thicknesses of muslin or one thickness of canton flannel. Prints need not be washed any longer than is necessary to free them completely from hypo. When running water is used for washing, the stream should not be allowed to fall directly on the prints as it will cause breaks in the fibre of the paper, producing blisters. Place a tumbler or graduate in the washing tray and allow the water to run into it and overflow into the tray.

A CONVENIENT ACCESSORY

Eastman Tray Siphon.

The Eastman Automatic Tray Siphon is an inexpensive device that converts an ordinary wash tray into a very effective washing machine. This siphon was invented by a scientist and it works on correct scientific principles—puts fresh water in at the top of the tray and siphons out the chemically laden water from the bottom, where it naturally settles, working entirely automatically.

The siphon may be adjusted to maintain the water at any desired level. The water coming into the tray makes a complete circuit, siphons out at the same speed it enters, and the force of the stream may be adjusted to keep the prints separated and in motion. There is also the assurance that the water will be changed every few minutes.

The Eastman Tray Siphon attaches to any water tap and is adjustable to any tray. Its efficiency and inexpensiveness make it an accessory every photographer who "does his own" should add to his workroom equipment.

208

TEST FOR HYPO

To determine when the print is thoroughly free from hypo, follow the directions on page 237.

DRYING VELOX PRINTS

After prints have been washed thoroughly remove from the wash water and place on a clean glass in a pile face down and press out some of the water. Then lay out separately, face down on cheesecloth stretchers. These may be constructed by making a framework of light wood and tacking unbleached cheesecloth tightly over it. Prints dried in this manner will curl very slightly.

If stretchers are not used, dry the prints face down on clean, uncolored cloth, or towels, which are free from lint.

Never dry Velox prints *between* ordinary blotters or on papers. They are likely to stick and cause much annoyance.

The Kodak Photo Blotter Roll offers an excellent means of drying prints and enlargements. The blotter material is covered with muslin so that prints will not stick and by placing them face down on the blotter they dry quite flat. A strip of corrugated board helps to circulate air through the roll. The Kodak Photo Blotter Roll is $11\frac{1}{2}''$ wide by 6 feet long and will take care of sixty prints of average size.

WHITE MARGINS

The Kodak Auto-Mask Printing Frame and the Kodak Amateur Printer are especially designed for making prints with white margins, see pages 217 and 216.

Kodaloid Printing Masks that include all of the popular sizes of negatives can be obtained. These very convenient masks are trans-

parent, are accurately cut and will produce excellent white margins.

Suitable masks can be made by cutting an opening the size of the desired print, from a sheet of black or opaque paper. Eastman Mask Charts, see page 210, are, however, much better. They are closely ruled, and therefore provide an easy and convenient means for making masks of any desired size.

Kodaloid Masks.

Eastman Mask Charts.

When ready to print, the mask is placed in the printing frame and the negative placed on top, or beneath the opening of the mask, with the back or shiny side of the negative next to the glass. Make sure that the transparent margin of the negative does not appear in the opening of the mask.

A sheet of Velox paper, which should be just a little larger than the opening cut in the mask chart, is then placed in position, and the back of the printing frame closed. Then proceed, in the regular way, with the making of the print, as described on page 203.

FOR ACCURATE TRIMMING

Staunchly constructed, in sizes suited to the every-day photographer's needs. The boards are of hard wood, the blades of fine quality steel, and the rules are plainly marked.

Kodak Trimming Board.

FOR DRY MOUNTING

Kodak Dry Mounting Tissue offers one of the most satisfactory methods of mounting prints. Just fix the tissue on the print, lay both on the mount, and press with a warm flat-iron. The heat causes the tissue to fuse, giving perfect contact between print and mount at every point. See directions, page 242.

Kodak Dry Mounting Tissue.

FOR PASTE MOUNTING

Kodak Photo Paste is an excellent white adhesive. It is made especially for mounting prints, and will not bleach or discolor them.

Kodak Photo Paste.

A HANDY AID

The inexpensive Flexo Print Roller, long a favorite with the amateur, has a four-inch rubber roll, supported in a black enamel frame.

Flexo Print Roller.

FOR A HIGHER GLOSS

Glossy Velox produces prints with a high gloss, particularly suited to negatives full of detail. A higher sheen is produced by the method with which the paper is dried. Take prints from the wash water and place face down on a ferrotype tin, squeegee into contact and allow to become bone dry, when they will peel off with the desired luster. Before using the tin it should be prepared as described on page 238.

SEPIA TONES ON VELOX

There are occasions when it is desirable to modify the tone of Velox prints, in order to secure some effect more in keeping with the subject than the original color produced by development only. The Sepia tone will not fade and may be secured by means of the Velox Re-development process which gives best results and yields pleasing, permanent tones.

Velox prints which have been evenly and thoroughly fixed and washed will give desirable results with the Re-developer, but some subjects, such as marines, night pictures, and snow scenes, are best rendered in black and white tones. Landscapes, autumn scenes, and portraits are given greater artistic values by the warmth of tone which the Re-developer produces.

A tube of Velox Re-developer consists of a bleaching powder and a re-developing powder. Each powder contains chemicals which require only the addition of water to make a bleaching bath for the reduction of the print before re-development, and a solution for re-development to a sepia tone. One tube of the Velox Re-developer is quite sufficient to re-develop about sixty 3¼ x 5½ Velox prints or their equivalent. It is important that the prints should have been thoroughly washed so that no trace of hypo remains. In order to obtain the best results it is advisable to have the prints dry before re-developing. Prepare the bleaching bath and re-developing solution according to the instructions given on the glass tube. Place the black and white print in the bleaching solution; let it remain until all trace of black has disappeared from the shadows, about one minute; it should then be removed and rinsed thoroughly in fresh water and placed in the re-developing solution, where the faint image immediately changes to a warm, brown tone, gradually deepening until all its former brilliancy returns, but in a sepia tone instead of black and white. This requires fully thirty seconds. Too strong a solution of Re-developer or too long immersion in this solution will cause blisters. After re-development rinse the prints, and immerse them in a hardening bath composed of Velox Liquid Hardener, 1 ounce (32 cc.); water, 16 ounces (500 cc.). Leave the prints in this solution for about five minutes. A final washing of about a half hour is then given.

Velox Re-developer will also produce excellent sepia tones on any bromide paper. The age of the print does not, seemingly, make any difference in the tones obtainable. The best results are obtainable from prints which have a good bluish-black tone, rather than a green or olive tone, such as is produced by the use of too much bromide. Both the bleaching and the re-developing baths will retain their strength for some time if kept in well stoppered bottles and it is advisable to keep them in a dark place when not in use.

A careful study of these instructions will enable you to produce satisfactory results on any surface of Velox or Bromide paper.

212

Splendid composition, excellent tone values.

CAUSES OF NON-SUCCESS

By consulting the following causes of failure you will probably be able to locate any trouble you may have.

PRINTS ARE TOO DARK.

Overexposure.

Overdevelopment.

Developer too warm; keep it at 70°F. (21°C.).

Negative too weak or thin.

Perhaps the wrong contrast of paper was used; try No. 3 or No. 4 Velox. If negative is very flat use No. 5.

PRINTS ARE TOO LIGHT, LACK DETAIL.

Underexposure or underdevelopment; developer too cold; keep it at 70°F. (21°C.); try Contrast No. 0 or Contrast No. 1 Velox.

GRAYISH WHITES THROUGHOUT ENTIRE PRINT.

Chemical or light fog, test the light (see page 200).

Insufficient Potassium Bromide in developer.

Too long development.

Old paper.

GRAYISH MOTTLED OR GRANULATED APPEARANCE OF EDGES OR ENTIRE PRINT.

Underexposure, forced development.

Old paper.

Moisture, paper kept in damp place.

Chemical fumes, ammonia, illuminating gas, etc.

GREENISH OR BROWNISH TONES, SOMETIMES MOTTLED.

Developer exhausted, badly discolored, or too cold.

Excess of Potassium Bromide.

Overexposure and underdevelopment.

BROWN OR RED STAINS.

Exhausted or oxidized developer. (Never use developer after it is much discolored or when too warm.)

Fixing bath lacks sufficient acid (sometimes milky) and prints were not moved occasionally to allow even fixing. (See page 206.)

PURPLE DISCOLORATION. (Not frequent.)

Prints not moved occasionally during fixing.

ROUND WHITE SPOTS.

Air-bells on the surface of paper.

To avoid, be sure to develop prints face up, immediately brushing off with the fingers any air-bells that may form. Use sufficient developer to cover the prints thoroughly.

ROUND OR IRREGULAR DARK SPOTS.

Caused by air-bells forming on the surface of print when several are allowed to become matted together in fixing bath, and failing to move prints about occasionally during fixing.

WHITE DEPOSITS ALL OVER SURFACE OF PRINT.

Milky Hypo bath. (Incorrectly mixed or impure chemicals used.)

YELLOWISH WHITES.

Stain all over print is result of underexposure and forcing development.

Prints not kept moving for the first few seconds after immersion in the hypo fixing bath.

Too weak a developer.

Insufficient fixing and washing.

Iron in wash water—may come from rust in water pipes.

Print exposed to air too much while developing, especially in warm weather. Use plenty of developer.

Sea air will affect Velox, causing yellow whites, so packages should not be left open and prints should be developed immediately after exposure.

The temperature of the developer is also important. A solution that is too cold will produce failures more readily than when it is used at the normal degree.

"SS" Pan Film negative, 1/350 second, stop f.5.6.

An enlargement from a portion of a miniature
negative made on Kodak Panatomic Film.

A PRINTER, FOR EFFICIENCY

Kodak Amateur Printer.

The Kodak Amateur Printer offers the maximum of printing efficiency with Velox or any developing-out paper.

The Printer consists of a box with a removable top, and in it a glass window through which the printing is done. Prints may be made with white margins, any size from $1\frac{5}{8}$ x $2\frac{1}{2}$ to 4 x $5\frac{1}{2}$ inches, by a simple automatic masking device, which holds the negatives firmly until released. Within the box is a small red electric bulb to permit the adjustment of negative and paper, and provision is made for a 60-watt electric lamp, which is automatically turned on to make the exposure when the hinged frame is closed. At the side of the box is a window covered with orange fabric. With the white electric lamp turned on, it serves as a safe light for developing Velox.

"SS" Pan Film negative, 1/50 second, stop f.8, Pictorial Diffusion Disk.

To operate the Kodak Amateur Printer it is necessary that electricity be available.

AN AUTO-MASK PRINTING FRAME

The Auto-Mask is the most convenient and useful printing frame that has yet been produced. It is adaptable to the printing of negatives of any amateur size from 4 x 5, $3\frac{1}{4}$ x $5\frac{1}{2}$ and smaller, using the same simple masking device employed on the Kodak Amateur Printer. The negative is held firmly in place by the mask and is readily released, when desired, by a slight pressure on the thumb lever.

Kodak Auto-Mask Printing Frame.

Any number of uniformly masked prints may be made without changing the position of the negative, and if desired, prints may be so made that white space is left at the side or bottom for writing. The scales attached to the stationary guides are an aid in getting the desired size of the mask openings.

CLOUDS IN THE PICTURE
By the Printing-in Method

While it is possible by using a Kodak Sky Filter to record clouds in the negative, as explained on page 90, you may have some landscape or marine negatives that were made on cloudless days, and prints from these might be improved pictorially, by the

A typical cloud negative.

addition of a cloud or two. Before attempting to add clouds to your landscapes by the printing-in process, it would be well to obtain a collection of cloud negatives in order that you may be able to select one that will fit each case, for it must be remembered that the clouded sky needed in each instance depends almost entirely upon the conditions existing at the time the landscape negative was obtained. For instance, should you picture a landscape when the sun is directly back of the camera and then print in from a negative, the clouds of which have received their illumination from immediately in front of the instrument, you can readily imagine the result, due to cross lights throughout the picture.

Then again, if the landscape is illuminated from the left, see that the clouds in the negative used are illuminated from the same point. Do not combine clouds taken on a sunless, gloomy day with a landscape taken when illuminated by the direct rays of the sun or vice versa.

Cloud negatives that are to be used for printing-in should be thin. They should, however, have sufficient strength to give brilliancy to the print. There are several advantages in using a cloud negative which is more or less transparent, as you can see through it and better judge as to its adjustment over the print to which you propose to add the clouds.

THE NEGATIVE

When obtaining negatives for printing-in, it is necessary to make very short exposures, because if we overexpose, even very slightly, we destroy the delicate contrasts that exist between the high-lights and shadows and thereby "flatten" the negative. For instance, if we make an exposure of $1/50$ of a second with stop $f.11$ for an ordinary landscape fully illuminated by the direct rays of the sun, we in most cases properly time the foreground but over-time the sky, destroying its beauty, and for that reason, when exposing for the sky alone $1/50$ or even $1/100$ of a second with stop $f.22$ will, in most cases, give proper recording.

An exposure thus obtained should be developed carefully, too much contrast avoided and development stopped the moment that full detail appears. You will then have a negative that will print rapidly and give you all the gradations of light and shade that were impressed upon the eye at the time the exposure was made. If a Kodak Color Filter is used, it will improve the cloud recording considerably.

THE PROCESS

In the first place, it is necessary, when printing the foreground, to obtain a white sky. In order to do so you must mask that portion of the

218

negative in order that the light may not penetrate the film and affect that part of the print underneath it. First take a sheet of thin cardboard and roughly sketch across its surface (about midway between the top and bottom) a mark to correspond as nearly as possible with the sky line of your negative; then cut your card along this line. Save both halves because you will need them later. Now procure a printing frame (containing a sheet of glass) somewhat larger than the negative you are to print from, and after locating the negative in the proper position, fasten it to the glass with small stickers, then tack the upper half of the cardboard to the face of the frame so that only that portion of the negative which you wish to print from will show. Cover the entire face of the frame with tissue paper and make your print.

Now place your cloud negative in the printing frame and properly locate the print over it, using the lower half of the cardboard to cover up the foreground so that the light will reach the sky only. It should be borne in mind that the cardboard (which we will call a mask or vignetter) when tacked on the frame should be raised from the glass about one-quarter of an inch, so that when printing, the light will diffuse and not produce a sharp line on your print. When using Velox, as the image does not show before development, it will be necessary to mark the paper at the edge in order to tell just where the sky line comes; otherwise you will be unable to properly locate your cloud negative. When using any developing-out paper it would be well to paste two or three thicknesses of tissue paper over your frame.

Clouds improve any scenic.   219

So much more detail is discernible in the big print. Delicate shadows broaden out, high lights become softer.

ENLARGING

ANY good little picture will make a better big one. Enlarging is a most interesting branch of photographic work and practically as simple as printing. Equipment is available to "fit" most any purse.

WHAT IS AN ENLARGEMENT?   HOW IS IT MADE?

An enlargement, in the usual sense, is a positive image or picture obtained by permitting rays of light to pass through a negative, then through a lens and focus on a sheet of sensitive bromide paper, which, after proper exposure, is developed, fixed, washed and dried in the usual manner, similar to an ordinary print. The size of the projected image depends upon the distance between lens and paper—the farther the lens is from the paper the greater the enlargement. This will be readily understood by reference to the diagram below.

An enlarged negative can also be made in the same manner by using a small *positive* in place of the negative, and projecting the image on a cut film or dry plate, instead of on Bromide paper.

ADVANTAGES OF THE ENLARGED PICTURE

The convenience of a small camera for the original exposure, plus the pleasure of large prints whenever desired, presents a combination that any picture maker will appreciate.

Enlargements have a great many advantages over contact prints. Whatever beauty or interest there may be in a small negative is brought out and emphasized by enlarging; frequently hidden beauty is revealed. Often just a portion of a negative, when enlarged, will make a very attractive picture by itself. Sometimes, too, the faces in a group picture are too small to be easily recognized. In such cases, if the negative is clear and sharp, an enlargement will overcome this objection. Again, there may be only a snapshot of a friend, whose portrait picture is desired. An enlargement will serve very satisfactorily. And, of course, enlargements, whether they are framed or not, make desirable pictures for the home or office and are especially attractive when colored.

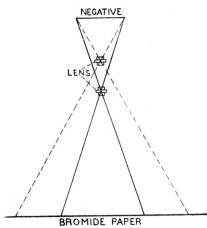

The farther the lens is from the paper the greater the enlargement.

The Kodak Auto-Focus Enlarger, Model B, in use.

The transition from the negative made with a small camera to the large print that tops your bureau or brightens your recreation room, wall or your desk is such an interesting one, and the process so easy and delightful, that big prints recommend themselves to any camera user as a logical photographic step.

THE KODAK AUTO-FOCUS ENLARGER MODEL B

The Kodak Auto-Focus Enlarger, Model B, capably meets the requirements of the every-day photographer and provides him with a practical and highly efficient instrument. All guess work in focusing is eliminated because an automatic focusing device is part of the Enlarger itself. This device slides on a vertical cam which causes levers to rack the bellows as the projector is raised or lowered, thus changing the focus the required amount. Therefore the Kodak Auto-Focus Enlarger is always in focus. The Photoflood Lamp provided with this Enlarger makes enlarging on bromide paper as rapid as contact printing and makes possible the use of many of the slower printing papers.

The construction of the Kodak Auto-Focus Enlarger is exceedingly simple, as can be seen from the illustration above. The slanting arm in which is incorporated a transformer and three-way switch to operate the printing lamp at "dim," "bright," and "no light," clamps to a table, shelf or other firm support. The slanting arm holds a vertical face-plate on which the projector slides. There is a graduated scale, so that the projector can be fixed at a point to make an enlargement of a given number of times the size of the negative, or the projector is simply moved up and down until any desired size is shown on the paper holder.

The projector consists of lamp house, negative holder, and bellows, and is equipped with a Kodak Anastigmat Lens. A sheet of flashed opal glass diffuses the light rays to just the proper degree, giving them more even distribution over the enlargement being made. The equipment includes seven flexible metal masks for use with popular sized negatives, and the new type paper holder.

The outfit is light and compact, but with all its simplicity it is exceptionally well made and sturdy.

For the benefit of amateurs who have the Kodak Auto-Focus Enlarger, Model A, in which the powerful Photoflood Lamp cannot be used, an adapter with a three-way switch is obtainable. This is attached to the metal arm of the Enlarger and connected to the lamp house by a flexible cord. It permits the use of the Photoflood Lamp, and the Model A Enlarger can then be operated in exactly the same manner as the Model B Enlarger described here.

WHAT THE KODAK AUTO-FOCUS ENLARGER WILL DO

This Enlarger will make sharp enlargements without attention to visual focusing. The negative holder has an opening of 4 x 6 inches. Enlargements may be from $1\frac{1}{2}$ to $3\frac{1}{2}$ times the dimensions of the negative used, or, in other words, from $2\frac{1}{4}$ to $12\frac{1}{4}$ times its area. Prints approximately $11\frac{1}{8}$ x $19\frac{1}{4}$ inches can be made from a $3\frac{1}{4}$ x $5\frac{1}{2}$-inch negative; $13\frac{7}{8}$ x $16\frac{1}{2}$ inches from a 4 x 5-inch negative and $4\frac{1}{2}$ x $6\frac{1}{2}$ inches from a half Vest Pocket negative ($1\frac{3}{16}$ x $1\frac{9}{16}$ inches).

The enlargement can be made from either a film or plate negative. The film can be either a separate negative or can be enlarged from while still in the strip, a slot being placed in either end of the negative holder for this purpose.

Once the negative is placed, the projector adjusted to give the desired size enlargement, and the paper placed in the holder, any number of prints can be made without further adjustments except to change the paper.

The Enlarger, because of its automatic focusing device, will always make the enlargement as clear and sharp as the original negative will permit. If this sharpness is not desired, a diffusing disc may be placed over the lens which will soften the lines considerably with-

The Kodak Home Enlarger in use.

out affecting the strength of the picture.

Both hands are free during this enlarging process, which gives ample opportunity for local control over the exposure by "shading" or "dodging" as explained on page 228. By a similar manipulation a particular part of a negative, such as a single figure or a head and shoulders, can be enlarged, vignetting or blotting out the rest of the negative—all of which is explained in detail in the instructions accompanying each Enlarger.

KODAK HOME ENLARGER

This is a very simple and inexpensive enlarger particularly adapted to the picture taker's own use. The lens is the sharp cutting Kodar 98 mm. assuring good definition and even illumination of the entire image field. A 60-watt Mazda Lamp furnishes the light. It enlarges up to approximately 11 x 14 inches from a 9 x 12 cm. negative (made with a No. 33 Kodak Recomar and slightly larger than a $3\frac{1}{4}$ x $4\frac{1}{4}$-inch negative). It enlarges to 5 x 7 inches from a half Vest Pocket size negative. A $3\frac{1}{4}$ x $5\frac{1}{2}$-inch negative will fit in the negative holder but only $4\frac{1}{2}$ inches of its length can be enlarged. Bromide paper must be used and the work done in a darkroom.

P.M.C. Bromide Paper is recommended because of its speed and the great variety of surfaces and degrees of contrast in which it is offered. See list on page 228.

The operation of this enlarger is extremely simple. A negative is placed in the holder which is put into the projector with its face or dull side towards the lens. When the light is switched on an image will appear on the easel. To make this image larger, move the projector away from the easel; to make the image smaller, move the projector towards the easel.

When you have adjusted the image to about the required size, examine it for focus, that is, sharpness and distinctness. If the image is indistinct, move the lens support back and forth until small details or fine lines in the picture are quite sharp and distinct. Then in a safe light the bromide paper is put behind the spring clips on the easel and the exposure made.

The camera and its stand move in a groove to adjust the image to the desired enlargement size. Moving the lens support in a second groove gives sharp focus.

THE KODAK MINIATURE ENLARGER

This new, versatile and moderately priced miniature enlarger accommodates negatives up to $2\frac{1}{4}$ x $3\frac{1}{4}$ inches (the maximum printable area is $2\frac{1}{4}$ x $2\frac{1}{2}$ inches) and focuses for enlargements of from $2\frac{1}{2}$ to 10 diameters.

Negatives in the strip can be handled as conveniently as a single film negative. The operation of the enlarger is extremely simple—adjustments for sizes of image are made by a simple movement of the sliding bracket up or down the face-plate, and sharp focus is quickly made by a turn of the knurled lens focusing mount.

Quite often a negative will have possibilities of making some other proportioned picture than shown in its entirety. The "picture found within a picture" can well be handled in the Kodak Miniature Enlarger because provision has been made to slide the whole negative holder sideways as well as to and from the operator. This permits placing the desired portion of the negative in the center of the enlarger.

This enlarger uses the Photoflood Lamp, making possible the use of a great variety of printing papers, and shortening exposure time very considerably.

Enlargements up to $11\frac{1}{2}$ x $14\frac{1}{2}$ inches with white margins are made on the paper holder, and considerably larger with the paper holder removed and the sensitive paper pinned to the table or floor.

The lens is a Kodak Anastigmat $f.4.5$, and the definition and quality of the image leave nothing to be desired.

NOTES ON ENLARGING

The work must be done in a darkroom, otherwise the sensitive paper will be fogged. The darkroom, to be safe, must be entirely free from white light, and of course can be more easily obtained at night. Ample illumination can be secured from a Brownie, Kodak, or Eastman Safelight Lamp. When equipped with a Series o or oA Safelight any of these darkroom lamps will produce a light which is suitable and quite safe for bromide or any other paper.

The negative which is to be enlarged from should be sharp, and neither excessively dense nor thin. To yield a large picture of good quality it should be free from imperfections, as spots, stains, pinholes and scratches, as these are greatly magnified in the enlargement.

MAKING THE EXPOSURE

The exposure should be such that the enlargement will require at least a minute and a half to develop to the proper depth under the conditions mentioned on page 232. If the print is too dark before that time, over-exposure is evident. Before making an enlargement, it is advisable to make a test to determine the proper duration of the exposure, as described in the manual accompanying the Enlarger.

A HANDY ENLARGEMENT EXPOSURE CALCULATOR

The Kodak Enlargement Exposure Calculator is a convenient accessory that shows subsequent exposure times once the exposure has been

determined for any given magnification. It consists of two metal scales, one revolving within
the other, and is designed for use with enlargers
having magnification scales and employing
diffusion illuminating systems (not condensers).

WHAT PAPER TO USE

Bromide paper is a rapid photographic paper,
coated with a highly sensitive emulsion composed principally of bromide of silver and gelatine. The emulsion is similar to that of the
ordinary film, though not as fast, and the paper can be developed in
a stronger light than would be safe for films.

Silver bromide gives a dense black tone after it is exposed to light
and developed, the unexposed portions of the sensitized paper remaining the color of the stock, white, pensé, buff, natural tint, or old ivory.

Bromide paper has remarkable keeping qualities, both before and
after exposure, and the developed print when carefully fixed and
washed is as permanent as the paper support itself.

KODABROM—The ideal enlarging paper for beginner or for the advanced worker who makes pictures of salon calibre.

It is definitely a new type high speed projection paper designed to
give a full scale of tones with brilliant, rich blacks. With normal exposure full density and brilliance are reached in but 45 seconds development. Wide lati-
tude is another prop-
erty inherent in this
paper. Kodabrom will
yield just as good a
print with an exposure
that requires 1½ min-
utes development.
This, of course, means
a lot to the amateur
who makes enlarge-
ments from negatives

Kodabrom Paper				
GRADE	SURFACE	COLOR	WEIGHT	DEGREES OF CONTRAST
E	SMOOTH Semi-matte	White	Double	1-2-3-4
F	GLOSSY	White	Single	1-2-3-4
F	GLOSSY	White	Double	1-2-3-4
G	FINE GRAIN Lustre	Natural White	Double	1-2-3-4
N	SMOOTH Lustre	White	Single	1-2-3-4
N	SMOOTH Lustre	White	Double	1-2-3-4
P	FINE GRAIN Lustre	Old Ivory	Double	1-2-3-4

227

of varying density. He cannot judge the exposure correctly every time but wants prints of uniform quality. Kodabrom will give that uniformity even with exposure variance. In addition to the convenience, this naturally prevents waste.

Kodabrom Paper is made in the grades, surfaces, colors, weights, and degrees of contrast shown in the table on page 227.

P. M. C. Bromide Paper—This paper is of excellent quality; it is furnished in a variety of stocks and surfaces, and several of the grades are made in two, three and four emulsions or degrees of contrast.

Among the somewhat slower fine quality papers are:

Vitava Opal—A paper of pleasing warmth of tone, a wide scale of gradation and with ample speed for enlarging with Photoflood Lamp equipment. Made in three weights of stock and several surfaces; a variety can be found for any subject.

Vitava Projection Paper—This is a fast paper which has fine portrait quality with slightly less warmth of tone than Opal. In two degrees of contrast and a number of surfaces.

LOCAL CONTROL

When making enlargements from negatives of varying quality the results can often be greatly improved by controlling the exposure time, allowing more or less exposure on different parts of the print.

Practically all negatives, excepting those that are badly under-exposed, or overexposed, contain much delicate detail that is scarcely noticeable in a small contact print, but is clearly seen in an enlargement.

The absence of detail in parts of the light or dark tones of a small picture is not displeasing, but in the case of an enlargement these areas, being larger, are much more conspicuous and would be improved if more detail could be obtained. If the negative shows detail in these areas it can be recorded in the enlargement, and, what is of even greater importance, the contrast between the various tones of the picture can also be increased or decreased as much or as little as desired by controlling the exposure locally, when making the enlargement. See illustration on page 230.

The lines leading from the lens to the paper suggest the size of the enlargement being made, and the small dark patch on the projected image represents an area that would appear too dark, or without detail in the enlargement if the light were allowed to act on it as long as on the other parts of the picture.

To control the exposure locally, allow the light to act on the whole picture as long as is necessary to fully print the dark tones. When these dark tones have been fully printed, hold a piece of cardboard in such a position between the lens and the paper that it prevents the light from reaching and consequently over-printing the part of the picture that has been fully recorded, without preventing it from reaching the parts that are not yet fully printed. The size of the cardboard must be

Exposure 2 *minutes, stop f*.6.3.

determined by the size of the area to be shaded, and by the distance the cardboard is held from the lens. The nearer it is to the lens the larger the shadow it will cast and the more diffused the edges of the shading will be in the finished picture. By holding it about midway between the lens and the paper, and by continually moving it a little while the shading is being done, no lines due to the shading will show in the picture.

The cardboard should be attached with gummed paper strips, or any other suitable medium, to a strip of clean glass about half-an-inch wide, and fully as long as half the length of the paper used. As the light will pass through this glass handle there will be no appreciable effect when shading or "dodging."

For printing detail in light tones a sheet of cardboard that will shade the entire paper should be used. A small hole must be cut in the cardboard through which the light passes during the shading. The area and shape of the hole can be changed by placing the fingers over part of it.

While somewhat difficult to describe, this is really an exceedingly easy process, and with a little practice the amateur should be able to obtain the results desired—results that cannot be excelled by any other method known. If a diffusion or softening of the lines of the entire picture is desired, this effect can be readily obtained with a diffusing disc. This is a specially prepared glass mounted in a round cell, and when it is to be used should be slipped over the lens of the Enlarger.

The diffusing disc does not change the focus, nor does it

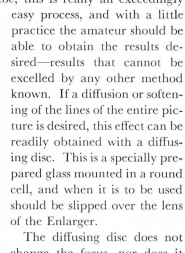

Local control or "dodging" when making the enlargement.

appreciably increase exposure. It merely softens the lines of the image.

When the negative is very sharp, especially in the case of landscapes, or negatives made with the Kodak Portrait Attachment of large head and shoulder portraits, the soft effect produced by the diffusing disc will be found pleasing and the result very artistic.

To remove objectionable background, around a figure for example, a sheet of cardboard with a hole in it may be so manipulated that only the rays of light that reproduce the figure pass through. The result is a vignette effect. The background can be entirely eliminated by blocking it out in the negative. To do this, all but the part to be enlarged should be painted with Eastman Opaque.

SPECIAL EFFECTS

Pictures of beautiful softness and breadth can be obtained by making the enlargement through a screen of silk bolting cloth. The screen softens the heavy mass of the shadows and blends them into harmony with the lighter tones.

The most convenient way to use bolting cloth is to stretch it over a frame. If it is used in contact with the paper, the enlargement has the appearance of being made on fine meshed canvas.

To secure diffusion, place the screen one-fourth inch to one inch from the paper. The farther the screen the greater the diffusion.

The use of the screen increases the exposure about one-third. A very fine quality of silk bolting cloth, for enlarging purposes, may be obtained through Kodak dealers.

Negatives which are to be enlarged through silk bolting cloth should have more than average contrast. The light lines made on the enlargement by the mesh of the cloth are almost invisible in the highlights, but in the shadows they introduce a certain amount of light tones, thus decreasing the contrast. A little experimenting will teach much.

DEVELOPMENT OF THE ENLARGEMENT

After the exposure has been made the next step is development. This is done in the same manner as the development of contact prints, except that the trays must be larger to accommodate the larger sized paper, and the time required for developing is a little longer.

Bromide and Vitava papers are not as sensitive to light as a film

and a somewhat stronger light may be employed for developing. The Series o or oA Safelight in the Brownie, Kodak, or Eastman Safelight Lamp, with a 10-watt bulb, gives a safe and suitable light for these papers. A small window opening into daylight, covered with two thicknesses of yellow post office paper, will also serve, as will an ordinary oil-burning darkroom lamp.

With the developer prepared according to directions at 70° Fahr. (21° C.), the image should appear in from 12 to 15 seconds. It requires at least 1½ minutes to complete the development.

Mealy, mottled prints indicate overexposure and short development.

"Flat" prints are caused by overexposure, under development, or by using a paper of the wrong degree of contrast.

Greenish tones indicate overexposure or too much potassium bromide in the developer.

After development is complete the print should be rinsed in clean water for a few seconds and then immersed in the fixing bath.

There are a number of developers that will produce good results on Bromide and Vitava papers, when handled by experienced persons who understand them. The professional photographer enlarges from negatives of uniform quality and for a certain effect. The amateur, on the other hand, finds his negatives varying in density and quality, and the best developer for him to use is the one affording the greatest latitude in exposure and development, and one that keeps well in solution.

The D-72 developer (which comes in prepared form) is recommended for Kodabrom. For P.M.C. papers use Nepera Solution, the M.Q. Tubes, the Eastman Universal Developer Tubes or the D-72 developer. *Vitava Opal and Vitava Projection Papers require the special formula D-52 on page 233.*

Prepare the developer, diluting it with water following the instructions packed with the paper. The temperature should be 70° F. (21° C.).

If you prefer to mix your own developer for Kodabrom or P. M. C. Bromide Paper the following formula is recommended.

Elon-Hydroquinone Developer (*Formula D-72*)*

Stock Solution

	Avoirdupois		Metric
Water (about 125° F.) (52° C.)...........	16	ounces	500.0 cc.
Elon...................................	45	grains	3.1 grams
Sodium Sulphite, desiccated, (E.K.Co.)....	1½	ounces	45.0 grams
Hydroquinone..........................	175	grains	12.0 grams
Sodium Carbonate, desiccated, (E.K.Co.)..	2¼	ounces	67.5 grams
Potassium Bromide.....................	27	grains	1.9 grams
Cold water to make....................	32	ounces	1.0 liter

For Kodabrom, use stock solution 1 part, water 2 parts for rapid development (45 seconds to 1 minute). If longer development is desired dilute 1 to 3 or 1 to 4 and add ¼ ounce (8 cc.) of a 10% solution potassium bromide to each quart (1 liter) of diluted developer.

For P.M.C., use stock solution 1 part, water 4 parts.

Develop at least 1½ minutes at 70 degrees F. (21° C.).

If greater contrast is desired dilute stock solution 1:2 or 1:1. With 1:1 dilution add 15 grains (1 gram) potassium bromide per 32 ounces (1 liter) of developer.

This concentrated developer will keep for several months in bottles filled to the neck and tightly corked.

For Vitava Opal and Vitava Projection Papers neither Nepera Solution nor Formula D-72 should be used. For these special papers use the following formula:

Elon-Hydroquinone Developer (*Formula D-52*)*

Stock Solution

	Avoirdupois		Metric
Water (about 125° F.) (52° C.)...........	16	ounces	500.0 cc.
Elon...................................	22	grains	1.5 grams
Sodium Sulphite, desiccated, (E.K.Co.)....	¾	ounce	22.5 grams
Hydroquinone..........................	90	grains	6.3 grams
Sodium Carbonate, desiccated, (E.K.Co.)..	½	ounce	15.0 grams
Potassium Bromide.....................	22	grains	1.5 grams
Cold water to make....................	32	ounces	1.0 liter

For Vitava Opal and Vitava Projection Papers, use stock solution 1 part, water 1 part.

Develop not less than 1½ minutes at 70 degrees F. (21° C.).

*These developers are available in prepared powder form for mixing with water to make 1 quart or larger quantities of solution.

ACID RINSE BATH

When a large number of prints are to be made, we recommend that they be rinsed between developing and fixing in an acid rinse bath for at least five seconds, as its action checks development and prevents staining troubles. It also permits a larger number of prints to be fixed before the fixing bath need be discarded because it prevents neutralization of the acid in the fixing bath by the alkaline developer.

ACID RINSE BATH (*Formula SB-1*)

	Avoirdupois	Metric
Water	32 ounces	1 liter
*Acetic Acid (28% pure) (E.K.Co.)	1½ fluid ozs.	48 cc.

*To make 28% acetic acid from glacial acetic acid, dilute 3 parts of glacial acetic acid with 8 parts of water.

Move or agitate the print while it is in the rinse bath to insure thorough access of the solution to all parts of the print. Use a fresh bath for each batch of prints because the acid will become neutralized by the alkaline developer carried in by the prints.

With a one to two seconds drain after development the equivalent of about twenty 8 x 10-inch prints may be processed in 32 ounces (1 liter) of the SB-1 bath, before it becomes alkaline and therefore useless.

FIXATION

234

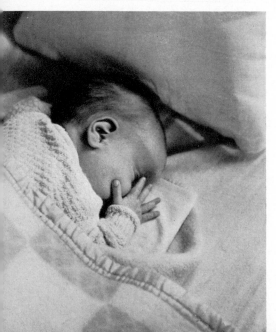

Fixation is of utmost importance as upon this depends, in a large measure, the permanence of the photographic print. Prepare the fixing bath with as much care as is given to the preparation of the developing solution.

When the prints have been rinsed thoroughly, immerse them in the fixing bath, page 235, for 10 to 15 minutes and agitate each print thoroughly.

The time necessary for fixation of prints depends largely upon the thoroughness of access of the

A picture that will grow in value with the years.

Note values in greens of foliage and water, also sky tones. Sail was brown. Panatomic negative.

fixing bath to the emulsion. Rapid fixing can best be induced by thorough agitation. Keep all prints immersed, otherwise bleaching of the image may occur. Trouble from stains and air-bells can be prevented if the prints are kept moving.

A fixing bath can be prepared using Kodak Acid Fixing Powder, or the following formula.

The Kodak Acid Fixing Powder is supplied in packages of different sizes, which contain all the chemicals necessary to prepare a correct acid fixing bath. Directions for preparing are given on each package.

ACID HARDENING FIXING BATH FOR PAPERS (*Formula F-1*)

	Avoirdupois	Metric
Sodium Thiosulphate (Hypo)	16 ounces	480 grams
Water	64 ounces	2 liters

When thoroughly dissolved, add four ounces (128 cc.) of Velox Liquid Hardener or the following hardening solution:

	Avoirdupois	Metric
Water (about 125° F.) (52° C.)	5 ounces	160 cc.
Sodium Sulphite, desiccated, (E.K.Co.)	1 ounce	30 grams
*Acetic Acid (28% pure) (E.K.Co.)	3 fluid ozs.	96 cc.
Potassium Alum (E.K.Co.)	1 ounce	30 grams

*To make 28% acetic acid from glacial acetic acid, dilute 3 parts of glacial acetic acid with 8 parts of water.

To make up the hardener, dissolve the chemicals in the order given above, using water at *about 125° F.* (52° C.). Be sure that the sodium sulphite has dissolved completely before adding the acetic acid. After the sulphite-acid solution has been mixed thoroughly, add the potassium alum and stir until dissolved completely. Add the cold hardener solution slowly to the cold hypo solution, stirring the latter continually.

It is important to note that the temperature of the fixing bath should never exceed 70 degrees F. (21° C.).

The above bath will fix approximately sixty 8 x 10-inch prints or their equivalent in other sizes if the acid short stop bath is used between development and fixation, or about thirty 8 x 10-inch prints or their equivalent if only a water rinse is used.

After all prints have remained in the fixing bath for a few minutes, the yellow shade may be removed from the light and the balance of the operation continued by ordinary light. Before turning on the white light, be sure that any unexposed or undeveloped sheets of sensitive paper are carefully protected from the light.

WASHING

When the prints are fixed, remove them, one at a time, from the fixing bath to a tray of clear water. To completely remove all traces of hypo, the prints must be washed for at least one hour in running water which flows rapidly enough to replace the water in the washing tray once every five minutes. Prints should be separated several times during this period. If running water is not available they should be washed in ten or twelve changes of water, allowing five minutes for each change. This is best done by using two trays, transferring the prints, one at a time, from one tray to the other and refilling with fresh water.

Prints will not wash free from hypo if they are piled in a heap in a tray, and the water simply runs in at one end and out at the other.

Enlarged from miniature negative. Taken from second floor window.

Whether washed by running water or by ten or twelve changes, the prints must be kept separated to allow the fresh water to reach both sides and remove all of the hypo.

If the running water is used, the stream must not be allowed to fall directly on the prints or it may break the fiber of the paper. Place a graduate or tumbler in the tray and let the water run into it and overflow into the tray. We recommend the Eastman Automatic Tray Siphon as the most efficient means for washing prints in the shortest possible time. See page 208.

Prints should not be washed longer than is necessary to free them entirely from hypo. This will be done if either of the methods outlined is faithfully carried through. Washing is equally as important as developing and fixing, and should receive the same careful attention for the best results.

HYPO TEST

To know when prints are entirely free from hypo, we recommend the following test:

Hypo Test (Formula HT-1a)

	Avoirdupois	Metric
Potassium Permanganate (E.K.Co.).......	4 grains	0.3 gram
Sodium Hydroxide (Caustic Soda)........	8 grains	0.6 gram
Water (distilled) to make...............	8 ounces	250.0 cc.

To make the test, take four ounces (125 cc.) of pure water in a clear glass and add one-quarter dram (1 cc.) of the Hypo Test solution. Pour one-half ounce (15 cc.) of the diluted solution into a clean one-ounce graduate or similar container. Take two 8 x 10-inch prints or their equivalent from the wash water and allow the water from them to drip for 30 seconds into the one-half ounce of test solution.

If a small percentage of hypo is present the violet color will turn orange in *about 30 seconds*, and become colorless in about one minute. In such case the prints should be washed further until no color change is produced, which indicates that the hypo has been reduced to a safe margin. This is shown by the violet color remaining unchanged when drippings from the prints are added to the Hypo Test solution.

Note: Oxidizable organic matter if present in the water reacts with the permanganate solution and changes the color in the same manner as hypo. The water should therefore be tested as follows:

When the first test is made with prints from the wash water, a similar test should be made with the tap water. Add a volume of tap water, equal to the wash water drained from the prints, to a second test solution prepared as above from pure water. If the sample to which tap water has been added remains a violet color, this indicates the absence of organic matter and it will be unnecessary to repeat the test. If the color is changed slightly by the tap water, the presence of hypo in the prints will be shown by the relative color change of the two samples. For example, if tap water sample turned pink and wash water sample became yellow, it would indicate the presence of hypo, while if both samples remained the same shade this would indicate absence of hypo.

DRYING

After thoroughly washing prints, they may be dried by laying them face down on uncolored cloths or towels which are free from lint.

Drying Glossy Bromide and Vitava Prints on Ferrotype Plates—The glossy surfaces of these papers can be made to produce a very high lustre by drying them on a ferrotype plate. After they have been washed place them face down on the plate, squeegee them into smooth contact and allow them to become entirely dry. They can then be readily removed from the plate and will have the desired lustre.

PREPARING FERROTYPE TIN

Before using the ferrotype plate it must be specially prepared to prevent the prints from sticking. To do this, dissolve ten grains of paraffin (the size of the tip of your little finger) in one ounce of benzine or gasoline and apply a little of this solution on a piece of canton flannel, covering the plate thoroughly and polishing off with a piece of dry flannel. The plate should be washed occasionally with hot water to remove any particles of gelatine that may remain on its surface. Eastman Ferrotype Plates may be obtained through any Kodak dealer.

UNCURLING UNMOUNTED PRINTS

Dry prints that have a tendency to curl may be kept flat by laying the *dry* print, face down, on a strip of cheesecloth attached to a piece of 3- or 4-inch pasteboard tube, then rolled up and left overnight. The prints will come out with a very slight *backward* curve.

This was enlarged from a section of a small nega-
tive Uninteresting and unnecessary area was masked.

SEPIA TONES ON KODABROM AND
P.M.C. BROMIDE PAPERS

Of the several processes for securing sepia tones in bromide prints, we recommend the method of re-developing and the use of Velox or Royal Re-developer or the formulas enclosed with the paper, for permanent results. There is no change, except in the color of the print, either in detail or gradation. The contents of one tube of Velox Re-developer are sufficient to re-develop about fourteen 7 x 11 prints or their equivalent. The time required is considerably less than when using any other method or toning process.

A bromide print of any texture of surface, which, when made, was *evenly fixed* and *thoroughly washed*, will give a desirable result when re-developed. Prints on buff stock paper produce the most pleasing sepias.

By following the directions given on the tube, a bromide print can be turned sepia in less than five minutes.

TO PREPARE SOLUTIONS WHEN USING THE
VELOX RE-DEVELOPER

A tube of Velox Re-developer contains chemicals which require only the addition of water to make a bleaching bath (for the reduction of the print before re-development) and a re-developing solution. Prepare the bleaching bath and re-developing solutions according to the instructions on the tube. (To prepare the solutions when using the Royal Re-developer follow the instructions as given on the package.)

For the best results the prints should be *dry* before re-developing.

DIRECTIONS FOR RE-DEVELOPMENT

1. Immerse the print in the bleaching bath, allowing it to remain until only faint traces of the half-tones are left and the black of the shadows has disappeared. This will take about one minute, though no harm will result from a somewhat longer immersion.

2. Rinse the print *thoroughly* in clean, cold water, until no yellowness remains in the wash water.

3. Place the print in the re-developing solution until the original detail returns. This requires fully thirty seconds.

4. After print has been re-developed, it should be rinsed *thoroughly* and then immersed for five minutes in a hardening bath of Velox Liquid Hardener, 1 part; water, 16 parts.

5. Wash the prints for about half an hour in running water, moving them about occasionally during the washing. If running water is not available, give the prints six changes of water, transferring prints separately from one tray to another, with an interval of about five minutes between each change.

For sepia tones on Vitava Projection and Vitava Opal Papers, follow the formulas and procedure as given in each package of the paper. If desired, the Hypo-Alum Toning Solution (Formula T-1a) may be used with the Vitava Opal Paper.

EMBOSSED WIDE MARGIN ENLARGEMENTS AND HOW TO MAKE THEM

Wide margins and a plate-sunk line around the picture make an especially attractive print for exhibition display or for framing. Such treatment gives the print a handsome finish particularly suited to pictures that are intended for home use or for gift purposes.

The matte, semi-matte and rough surfaces of enlarging papers are the most desirable for this kind of enlargement. Any of the double weight papers, in these surfaces, will do.

It is necessary to decide in advance upon the sizes of the prints to be made, because a mask and a form must be made for each size. For instance, if the mask is $3 \times 5\frac{1}{8}$ for a $3\frac{1}{4} \times 5\frac{1}{2}$ negative, this will make a $5\frac{1}{4} \times 9$-inch enlargement on an 11×14 sheet of paper. By leaving a two-inch white margin at top and sides and a two and one-half inch margin at the bottom, excellent proportions will be obtained and there will be room all around for trimming.

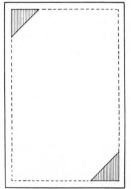

The embossing form is very easy to make.

For the size mentioned, the embossed line should be about three-eighths of an inch from the top and sides of the print and five-eighths from the bottom. The embossing form will therefore be 6 x 10 inches. It should be the same thickness as your print; consequently an old enlargement may be used for making your form. Draw a line three-eighths of an inch from top and sides and five-eighths from the bottom as shown in diagram, and cut out two of the corners as indicated by the dark triangles. These openings are used to locate the corners of your print when you are embossing.

Prints should be carefully spotted and flattened for embossing. Moisten the backs evenly to the edges with a solution of equal parts of wood alcohol and water and place between cardboards or blotters under pressure. If not allowed to become bone dry, the prints will lie perfectly flat and emboss without cracking.

Since it is necessary to see through the print to locate it over the form, make a 16 x 20-inch frame, four inches high, place a piece of clear or ground plate glass over the top and one or two lamps beneath.

Lay the form on the plate glass over the light. Place the print, face down, over the form, locating the corners of the picture in the triangular openings. Hold the print firmly and run an embossing tool or orange-wood stick over the back of the print, following the edge of the form. A brick covered with several thicknesses of paper makes an excellent weight to hold the print in place. If the pressure of the embossing tool is even, the result is a distinct plate-sunk line that adds materially to the effectiveness of the print.

MOUNTING

A very satisfactory way for mounting small enlargements, not larger than 6½ x 8½, is by the use of Kodak Dry Mounting Tissue. By using it the print is held flat and does not curl even on thin mounts. Prints larger than 6½ x 8½ are best mounted wet with a good starch paste or Eastman Photo Paste, as a Kodak Dry Mounting Press, which is really professional equipment, would be necessary with the tissue in the large sizes.

The tissue comes in flat sheets. It is not sticky, is easy to handle, and being waterproof protects the print from any impurities in the mount stock.

The process of mounting is as follows:

Lay an untrimmed print face down and tack to the back of it a piece of tissue, the same size or slightly larger, by applying the point of a heated flatiron to each end of the tissue. The iron should be just hot enough to melt the tissue, not so hot that it glides or so cold that it sticks. If too hot, it is liable to discolor the print.

Turn the print face up and trim print and tissue to the desired size, now lay the print in place on the mount or album leaf, cover it with a piece of clean white paper and press the whole surface with the hot flatiron for a few seconds; the time required depends upon the heat of the flatiron. *Press, don't rub.*

To Mount Prints with Paste—After the dry prints are trimmed, immerse them in a tray of clean water, allowing them to remain long enough to become thoroughly limp. Remove a wet print and place it face down on a table covered with oilcloth or a sheet of glass, and squeegee out any surplus water. Then brush over the back with Eastman or Kodak Photo Paste, working it in thoroughly; lift the print by the opposite corners, turn it over and place it in proper position on the mount. Lay a clean dry blotter over the print and press into contact with a squeegee or print roller. Lint, fuzz or surplus paste on the print should be immediately wiped off with a damp cloth or sponge.

To Mount Prints with Glue—In mounting prints on an album leaf or other sheet of fairly thin stock, it is often advisable to use glue instead of paste. In this case the prints should be mounted dry. Reverse a print, apply a very small amount of Kodak Liquid Glue to the corners only, turn the print over and press the glued corners carefully into contact with the sheet. Used in this way the glue will give very satisfactory results, whereas mounting the prints with paste on a thin sheet would result in unsightly distortion of both print and mount.

COLORING ENLARGEMENTS

The various surfaces of P. M. C. Bromide, Eastman Portrait Bromide, and Vitava Papers are particularly well adapted for coloring, and prints may be made very attractive through the many beautiful effects obtainable by the use of the Kodak Transparent Oil Colors or Velox Transparent Water Color Stamps referred to on page 244. Full directions accompany each set of colors.

Delicate shadows were registered on the Verichrome negative.

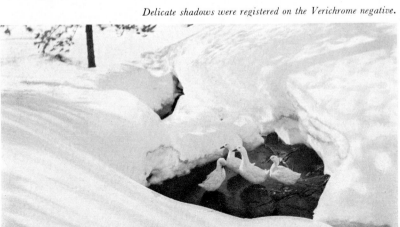

243

COLORING

Your photographs can be made much more attractive by the addition of color. Enlargements as gifts, prints for home-made calendars, or for the album, Christmas and birthday greetings made up from your own negatives, may be easily colored with Velox Transparent Water Colors or Kodak Transparent Oil Colors. You do not have to be naturally skilful with the brush. If you will follow with reasonable care the directions accompanying the color sets and the suggestions that follow, you will be able to produce very attractive pictures in full color.

TRANSPARENT WATER COLORS

Velox Transparent Water Colors.

These colors, 12 in a book, and twenty-six stamps to the sheet, are prepared for application either by tearing off one stamp (a small portion of the sheet which is perforated), and dissolving away the color in water in one of the compartments of the palette or by touching a wet brush to the sheet and removing as much of the color as needed. If a large quantity of any color is desired this may be mixed in tumblers.

Explicit directions are furnished with each sheet of color as to its application. The inside of the cover of the enameled box serves as a mixing palette. All you need after procuring the Velox Water Color Outfit are a few sheets of white blotting paper and a small roll of absorbent cotton.

The prints should be held flat while coloring by pinning to a drawing board or to a heavy mounting board by means of thumb tacks or glass push pins. The print surface should be moistened slightly by rubbing gently with a moistened cotton pad.

Below are subjects for coloring listed for the beginner in an order indicating the relative difficulty involved. A simple landscape, without people, is the easiest and a portrait the most difficult.

1. Simple Landscapes
2. Seascapes
3. Waterfalls and Landscapes
4. Still Life (fruits, flowers, etc.)
5. Group Pictures
6. Sunsets

The fundamental principles involved are the same in every case.

IMPORTANT POINTS

While directions are given with each set of colors, there are important methods of procedure to bear in mind. The diagram below and the numbered picture on page 246 are particularly useful.

Prints with a smooth *semi*-glossy surface, such as Velvet Velox, take the colors very well. Glossy surfaces are most difficult to color and should be avoided. Dead matte prints although less difficult to color than glossy prints are seldom satisfactory when colored. A smooth or rough semi-matte surface is very satisfactory for coloring.

Prints with considerable shadow detail, the darkest areas of which are gray-black rather than deep black, are usually the most suitable for water coloring. "Flat" prints (those which lack brilliance) often appear washed out when colored and contrasty prints show patchy black areas in the denser portions of the colored picture.

A necessary precaution is to keep the face of the print free from any greasiness, such as that caused by finger marks, otherwise the water colors will not "take" evenly on the print. Also, if the print has been hardened excessively by fixing in an acid hardening bath it will not color well. This difficulty may be overcome by treating the surface of the print with a five per cent solution of ammonia (common household ammonia may be used by diluting one part with ten parts of water); then wash the surface with several tufts of cotton wet with water.

SIMPLICITY OF COLOR BLENDING

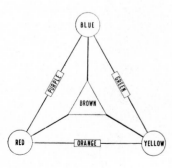

Mixing colors will be simplified if it is borne in mind that the tints required are varying combinations of the three primary colors—red, yellow and blue (strictly speaking, primary red is termed "Magenta" and primary blue "Blue-Green," but for simplicity we have termed them as above). The adjoining diagram indicates the colors obtained by mixing any two colors or by mixing

245

all three. Variations may be produced by adding together more or less of any of the primary colors; thus for orange, mix yellow and red; for green, mix yellow and blue; for purple, mix blue and red; and for brown, mix yellow, blue and red. Diluting the colors or mixing the secondary colors, orange, green or purple, in different proportions will give a still wider range of tones. To facilitate easier coloring the set of Velox Transparent Water Colors contains several colors which might be obtained by mixing two or three of the primary colors.

AN EXAMPLE

To better understand the method of procedure when applying the color, instructions will be given for coloring the photograph on this page, with the numbered tone areas. In this picture, there are only three primary subjects for coloring to be considered, namely, water, rocks, and trees. The picture may be colored using only two colors, a medium warm brown for the rocks and a moderately dark green for the trees and bushes, or it may be treated in detail by coloring every portion, such as the distant mountainside, the rock shadows, the

A typical scenic picture, suitable for coloring. The numbered areas are referred to on pages 247, 248.

patches of sunlight on the leaves and rocks in the right foreground, and so on. In every case in the following description the color was applied *weakly* and then gradually built up until the desired depth of color had been obtained. For simplicity in reference the various areas to be colored have been numbered.

1. A wash of light blue is added to the distant canyon above the waterfall as a basis for the purple haze characteristic of such canyons. Touches of blue are washed on the shadows in the falls and in the eddies around the rocks in the rapids.

2. The rocks are next in order and here great care must be exercised because brown usually dries down to a tone different from what is expected. The color should preferably be mixed by taking, first, a solution of warm brown, and then adding red, yellow, and blue, or stone gray to it until the desired tone is obtained. For the lighter, sunlit areas on the rocks, a medium light brown with a tinge of yellow is most effective. A later wash of green as subsequently mentioned under 5 will help produce the mossy appearance so often seen on boulders in streams. The most important point is, however, to keep the color *weak* so that it will blend evenly with the rest of the scene.

3. On the shadow portions of the rocks, add a deeper chocolate brown prepared by mixing dark blue, scarlet, and dark green with warm brown. Before coloring the area in question, test the shade by painting a spot near the edge of the picture where it will be trimmed off when the coloring has been completed.

4. For the bushes and leaves of trees which are bathed in warm sunshine, a wash of foliage green or even yellow in the extreme highlights gives the most pleasing effect. If the color is too yellow when applied it may be made more natural by a wash of light blue.

5. For the darker, shaded areas of the trees or where a tree stands out in silhouette, as at the base of the falls, deep green may be liberally applied, taking care to keep closely within the dark areas. A wash of green over the rocks will tone down the brown and add a mossy effect.

6. The coloring is now almost completed, but a few more touches will add to the picture's beauty and require only a little skill in application. On the sunlit spots in the leaves of the trees on the right and on the rocks just under the trees, the addition of a medium shade of yellow will brighten up these isolated points. Too much color must not be applied

or undue attention will be drawn to these spots which will detract from the central point of interest, the waterfall.

7. An ingenious method of accentuating the objects in the foreground is to apply a wash of dilute violet to the area around the edges of the rocks and bushes or leaves of the trees. The haziness of distance, in the canyon above the falls, will be improved by a wash of dilute violet.

Final touches are always necessary to tone down some regions of the picture and freshen up others, but these must be left to the discretion of the individual. If too much color has been added it may be softened with a tuft of cotton moistened with five per cent ammonia.

SUGGESTIONS FOR THE BEGINNER

Use *weak* or *dilute* colors, building up to the desired shade by successive applications.

Use daylight or "daylight" incandescent bulbs when coloring.

Certain colors must be allowed to dry before another color is added to the print, whereas other tones will give best results when added while the previous color is still wet. A little experience will help you to master the blending of colors.

If clouds are in the picture, they may be left white by running blue around them. It is possible with practice to create white cloud effects by leaving irregular patches of white when coloring the sky. Dark clouds are best left uncolored. If an evening effect is desired, do not use blue color, but tint the spaces between the dark clouds with pale yellow and add a light flesh tint around the edges of clouds, shading into the yellow.

If too strong a color has been used, it may be softened in two ways: (1) by washing with some neutral color such as stone gray, or (2) by gently rubbing with a tuft of cotton moistened with water or with a five per cent solution of ammonia. In emergency cases, the color may usually be entirely removed by soaking the print for a few minutes in the ammonia solution and then washing.

If the print surface repels the application of any color, it should be moistened with several applications of five per cent ammonia using a cotton swab. After treatment with ammonia water, the surface of the print should be moistened several times with plain water to eliminate most of the alkalinity.

Always keep the print moist while coloring, because more even blending as well as easier application of color will result. Use weak colors for distance and stronger colors for foreground work. Strong colors should not, however, be too brilliant, as the print will then appear gaudy.

TRANSPARENT OIL COLORS

Kodak Transparent Oil Colors.

These perfected oil colors are especially suitable for coloring photographs as they contain no element that might bleach or otherwise affect photographic paper. The set as shown at the left contains fifteen standard colors, which when mixed according to the chart in the instruction book accompanying them will produce practically any tint or shade that is desired. The outfit includes Sizing Fluid, Cleaning Fluid, a medium for thinning, a quantity of prepared cotton, skewers, and complete instructions. While all necessary information is given in the booklet, the following paragraphs contain decidedly helpful information for those who intend to take up the art of oil coloring.

The beginner will do well to study natural color. He should not forget that this entails, first, observing actual colors in nature, and second, "organizing" and visualizing the color on the print. For example, suppose he photographs a corner of a garden containing many bright, blush-red (magenta) flowers, against a background of very green leaves. A print of this, colored "truthfully" might be very unpleasant because magenta and green are complementary, and both are present in large areas so that they compete with each other violently. In a case like that we modify the color scheme in the interests of harmony, staying, of course, within the limits of probability in nature.

Thus, we could color the green leaves less intensely than they appeared, introducing bluish-green highlights and tending toward violet or brown in the shadows. In other words, we should arrange to have as little pure green in them as possible. Then they would not produce a discord with the flowers but would accentuate the intensity of the magenta without dividing our attention.

The full strength of oil colors is obtainable on the matte surface papers. The semi-matte and lustre papers can also be used quite satisfactorily, but the colors obtained will be in a slightly lighter scale. No priming or preparation of the surface is needed with Kodak Transparent Oil Colors for these papers. For general purposes a black and white print, on a white or near-white stock, will be most suitable. If anything like the effect of nature is desired, the shadows in the enlargement should never be black. Even deep shadows have a slight tinge of color, and it is difficult to make color show over a dense black. While working for gray shadows in the print, one must be careful that the highlight detail is not lost.

THE PALETTE

The palette should be white and reflecting. A convenient arrangement is a piece of glass laid on a sheet of white paper, or a piece of white "flashed" glass, at least 8 x 10 inches. The colors are squeezed out as needed near one edge of the palette, and the mixing is done on the remaining part. A small flexible palette knife is convenient for mixing colors. After the work at hand is completed the palette should be completely cleaned with the cleaning fluid.

HOW TO APPLY THE OIL COLORS

At first the beginner should confine himself to only the colors and the Transparent Medium in the large tube, and disregard the Sizing Fluid. Briefly, simply take a print and rub colors onto the surface, lightening them as desired by reducing the strength with Transparent Medium.

These oil colors can be removed completely by use of the special cleaning fluid, leaving the print perfectly clean.

Most of the actual coloring is done with absorbent cotton. With a little practice you can wrap a small tuft of cotton on the end of one of the pointed sticks so that it properly covers the point and does not come off easily. Moistening the lower part of the tuft with thumb and forefinger while wrapping it around the stick is a good way to make it hold on. The wad must be changed for every change of color unless they are to be mixed. For the larger areas a tuft of cotton is rolled into a pad and held between the fingers. The color should be applied only with the lower part of the pad and the fingers need not become soiled.

Time will be saved by smearing the color on more heavily than wanted, then wiping away the excess with clean, dry cotton. Wipe toward the center, that is, away from the edge of the part you are working on; in this way the color will not be dragged over the edge. For this wiping, the cotton can be used rolled up and held with the fingers and only for fine detail need be wrapped on a stick. The color should be used strong enough so that all excess can be wiped off the print, leaving a perfectly even film of color. This is the secret of evenness in oil coloring. Unsightly and unevenly applied color is the result of reducing too much, forcing one to leave the color in a heavy film, which is very difficult to apply evenly.

To remove color while it is still soft, apply Transparent Medium on the part, rub it into the color with cotton, then wipe off with clean cotton. If a full strength color is to be used on the cleaned part, apply the second color, wipe down, apply again and wipe off the excess.

In many pictures there are small parts surrounded by large areas of contrasting color. Thus, in portraits there are the eyes and probably jewelry, in landscapes perhaps a few bright leaves against a dark background, in gardens isolated flowers. It is not necessary to laboriously apply colors all around the edges of these things. It is better to let the surrounding color go all over them at first, then after this has been wiped down evenly, remove the color from the small contrasting spots with Transparent Medium, and then color them correctly.

For spots that are too minute for a cotton pledget, one can apply a little color on the point of a small brush. In this case, the color may be thinned with a small quantity of Sizing Fluid.

The application of special colors in the shadows adds life and realism far beyond the effect supplied by photographic shadows alone. For this purpose two very useful specially mixed colors are furnished: Flesh Shadows Warm and Flesh Shadows Cool.

PAT POINTS TO REMEMBER

Avoid the use of highly glossy surfaced papers.

Do not *over* color a picture—avoid vivid contrasts.

The print or enlargement should show good detail in the shadows with all darker portions of the print gray rather than black.

All prints for coloring should be well washed and free from Hypo. Oil coloring should be done by daylight, but may be done at night if a blue Mazda "daylight" lamp is used.

Rarely in oil coloring is the use of a brush necessary. For large areas, use a tuft of cotton. For small areas or detail a bit of cotton on a pointed stick should be employed.

The general rule for coloring landscapes is to color the more remote portions first, gradually working into the fine details. Far distant hills and mountains use tints of blue and purple. For massed trees of forests in the distance, use a blue-green. Trees in the foreground must be carefully colored with attention to detail. Grass or leaves in the foreground, light green, work in yellow in spots and deep green in others. To represent fall coloring, Raw Sienna, Flesh Shadows Cool, and Scarlet are used. Sunlit spots are always yellower. Be sure to use enough Transparent Medium or the grass and foliage will look unnatural and unpleasant.

Refer frequently to the "Guide to Colors and Mixtures" in the instructions with Kodak Transparent Oil Colors.

The secret of *evenness* in oil coloring is to originally apply the colors in sufficient quantity so that all excess can be wiped off leaving a perfectly even film of color of the correct depth.

Above the "cotton batting" clouds. To include a landing wheel of your plane helps to tell the story. 1/100 second, f.22 "SS" Pan Film.

Glossary of Photographic Terms

ABERRATIONS: The defects of a lens.

ABRASION MARKS: Black lines or markings produced on the surface of photographic paper by rubbing or pressure.

ACCELERATOR: A chemical added to a developer to bring out the image more quickly—sodium carbonate is commonly employed.

ACHROMATIC: Colorless; applied to a lens whose chemical and visual foci coincide.

ACTINIC: Applied to light which affects photographic films, plates and paper.

AIR-BELLS: Bubbles on sensitized surface of prints, produced by immersing the paper face down in the developer or using too small an amount of solution. This also applies to films and plates.

ANASTIGMAT LENS: One free from astigmatism, or the fault of not bringing vertical and horizontal lines equally well to a focus.

APERTURE: Applied to a lens opening.

BATH: A term applied to a developing, fixing or other solution.

BUBBLES: See Air-bells.

CHALKY: Term applied to prints showing excessive contrasts.

COMPOSITION: The arrangement or grouping of objects within the picture area to make a pleasing, harmonious general effect.

CONCENTRATED: As applied to liquid preparations means that the chemicals which comprise them have been dissolved in the least possible quantity of water.

CONTACT PRINT: A print made by placing the paper in contact with the negative.

CONTRASTY: A term applied to prints; meaning hard, "chalky," extremely black shadows and white highlights; lacking in detail as applied to negatives.

CONVERTIBLE LENS: One in which the two component glasses (front and rear elements) can be used as separate lenses.

COVERING POWER: The limits within which a lens is capable of giving a well defined image.

CURVATURE OF FIELD: A defect in a lens showing sharper definition at the center of the plate than at the edges.

DEFINITION: Clearness and sharpness of image.

DENSE: Applied to negatives which have been overexposed, overdeveloped or both.

DENSITY: The degree of opaqueness of a negative.

DEPTH OF FIELD: The distance from the nearest to the farthest point that is "in focus" or sharply defined in a picture.

DESICCATED: Anhydrous. Dry powder, not crystals. Applied to chemical salts from which all water has been removed.

DETAIL: The definition recorded by a lens of the minute parts of a subject.

DEVELOPER: A chemical solution employed to bring out or render visible the latent image on films, plates or paper.

DEVELOPING-OUT PAPER OR D. O. P.: Sensitized paper upon which the photographic image is invisible until development has taken place.

DEVELOPMENT: The process of converting the latent or invisible image on a film, plate or paper into a visible image.

DIAPHRAGM OPENING OR "STOP": The opening which admits light, through the lens, to the film.

DIFFUSED LIGHT: Such as comes from a clouded sky, in contra-distinction to direct sunlight. Light which does not strike directly, but is arrested and diffused by some medium, such as ground glass.

DIFFUSION OF FOCUS: Lack of "hair line" sharpness in a picture, producing a pleasingly soft effect.

DISTORTION: An incorrect rendering of the image—out of shape.

DODGE: To "dodge" or shade is to prevent light from striking a portion of a negative when printing by shading that portion with some opaque body.

EMULSION: A term applied to the light-sensitive coating on films, plates or paper, which is acted upon by the light rays.

EQUIVALENT FOCUS: The distance from the optical center of a lens to the ground glass when focused on a distant object.

EXPOSURE: The period of time during which a sensitized film, plate or paper is exposed to the action of light.

FERROTYPE PLATE: A highly polished enameled plate of thin metal used for obtaining a high gloss on prints, by drying the print with its face or emulsion side in contact with the plate.

FINE-GRAIN: Applied to the emulsion of a negative material. One that yields big enlargements having contact print quality.

FIXING: The process of removing the unacted upon silver salts from a negative or print, usually by immersing in a solution of hypo.

FLARE SPOT: A circular patch of light in the center of the image caused by a defect in the lens.

FLAT: Lack of vigor or contrast in a negative or print.

FLATNESS OF FIELD: That quality in a lens affording sharp impressions at both center and edge of negative.

FOCUS: The point at which converging rays of light from a lens meet, forming an image. A picture is said to be "in focus" when all details of the image are sharp and well defined.

FOCUSING SCALE: A graduated scale for different distances, which permits of focusing for any given distance, without using a ground glass screen.

FOCUSING SCREEN: A sheet of ground glass on which the image is focused and composed before exposure.

FOG: A deposit of metallic silver over the film or plate including those parts which should not have been affected by light. (See also Light Fog.)

FORCING: Attempting to bring out detail in an underexposed film, plate or print by prolonged development or by the addition of an accelerator—liable to produce fog.

FRILLING: The puckering up and detachment of the emulsion from the support around the edges; happens oftenest in hot weather, or through too much alkali in the developer.

GENRE: Genre pictures are those of every-day incidents — human interest pictures that tell a story — pictures that are illustrative of common life.

GRADATION: The range of tones from the highest lights to the deepest shadows in negatives or prints.

HALATION: A blurred effect, resembling a halo, usually occurring around bright objects; caused by reflection of rays of light from the back of the negative material. (Verichrome,"SS" Pan, Super X Pan and Panatomic Films are coated on the back with a special dye to prevent halation).

HALFTONES: All gradations between highlights and deepest shadows.

HARDNESS: Excessive contrast in negatives or prints, too great difference between lights and shadows.—See Contrasty.

HIGH KEY: A print is said to be in a "high key" when there are few gradations of tone, none of which is very dark.

HIGHLIGHTS: The portions of a picture upon which the greatest amount of light is concentrated. The denser portions of a negative or the lightest parts of a print.

HYPO: The abbreviation of the term Sodium Hyposulphite, or more correctly, Sodium Thiosulphate, used for fixing films, plates and paper.

IMAGE: The picture on a negative, on enlarging paper or as seen on the ground glass focusing screen.

INFINITY: A lens is said to be set for infinity when focused at a point beyond which all objects are sharply defined.

INTENSIFICATION: Increasing the density of a negative or print by the use of chemical solutions.

LATENT IMAGE: The image recorded upon a film, plate or paper by light action, and which is invisible until chemically treated by the process known as development.

LATITUDE OF EXPOSURE: That quality in a film or plate which allows variations in exposure without detriment to negative quality.

LENS: A circular glass or combination of glasses optically ground and polished, mounted in a metal cell.

LENS SPEED MARKING SYSTEMS: Diaphragm, or stop openings are marked in two systems, both based on the fundamental ratio of lens opening diameter to lens focal length. In the "f." value system the opening is expressed as a fraction of lens focal length, thus, "$f.8$" means the aperture is $1/8$ of focal length, "$f.16$," $1/16$ and so on. In "U.S." or Uniform System, the numbers are proportional to the exposure required. "$f.4$" being taken as unity: comparison follows

F. $f.4$ $f.4.5$ $f.5.6$ $f.6.3$ $f.8$ $f.11$ $f.16$
U.S. 1 1.26 2 $2 1/2$ 4 8 16

The markings 1, 2, 3 and 4, on some single lens folding cameras are merely arbitrary figures though they correspond, roughly, with $f.11$, 16, 22 and 32.

LIGHT FILTER: A colored glass, or stained film, used on or between the lens to absorb rays of certain colors and allow others to pass through.

LIGHT FOG: A graying of the image, produced by an unsafe darkroom lamp, or accidental exposure to white light.

LOW KEY: A print is said to be in "low key" when the few tones in it are mostly at the dark end of the scale.

MILKY: Appearance of an incorrect fixing bath. Often the result of using impure chemicals or improper mixing.

MOTTLED: Irregular spots on negatives or prints.

NEGATIVE: A photographic image on a film or plate in which the dark portions of the subject appear light, and the light portions dark.

NON-ACTINIC: Those colors or rays of light which do not affect certain light-sensitive photographic emulsions.

ORTHOCHROMATIC: Color sensitive. A film or plate is said to be orthochromatic when it is sensitive to colors of the spectrum other than the blue and ultra-violet to which all negative materials are especially sensitive. (Kodak Verichrome Film is orthochromatic.)

OVERDEVELOPMENT: Too long a time in the developing solution.

OVEREXPOSURE: Too long an exposure of the light-sensitive material.

OXIDATION: As applied to developer—a deterioration due to the presence of oxygen. An oxidized developer is dark in color and usually causes discoloration of the negative or print.

PANCHROMATIC: A film sensitive to *all* colors, recording them more in the relative brightnesses as seen by the eye. (Kodak "SS" Pan Super X Pan and Panatomic Films are panchromatic.)

PERSPECTIVE: The proportion of parts of a picture to one another in relation to distance.

PIN HOLES: Minute spots or holes in a negative, usually caused by dust settling on the surface before exposure.

POSITIVE: Opposite to a negative; the true picture.

PRECIPITATE: A substance which, having been dissolved, is again separated from its solvent and settles to the bottom of the vessel containing it.

RACK AND PINION: A screw and rack adjustment for focusing.

RECTILINEAR LENS: One which does not distort or show curvature of straight lines in the image.

REDUCER: A chemical solution for decreasing contrast or density.

REFRACTION: The change in direction of rays of light when passing through a transparent medium.

RESTRAINER: A compound or solution that will check or hold back the action of the developer.

RETOUCHING: The removal or softening of defects in a negative, by the application of pencil lines or color.

REVERSAL: The image or portions of it are positive instead of negative or vice versa. Caused by extreme over-exposure or exposure to white light of negative or print during development.

SHADOWS: The thinner or lighter portions of a negative or the darker portions of a print.

SHUTTER: The device on a camera which opens and closes to admit light to the sensitive film.

SOFT: Term applied to print or negative; refers to lack of brilliancy or contrast. A "soft" print will contain all possible detail.

SPHERICAL ABERRATION: A lens defect—the inability to bring the marginal and central rays of light to one focus, resulting in a loss of sharpness.

SPOTTING: The filling-in of spots or imperfections in a negative or print by means of india ink or spotting color with a fine brush.

SQUEEGEE: Usually a strip of soft rubber set in a handle, or a rubber roller, and used to place a print in contact with the ferrotype plate.

THICK: (See Dense.)

TONE: The shade, hue or degree of color prevailing in a negative or print. Also depth or intensity of any part of a photograph.

UNDEREXPOSURE: Too short an exposure for correct results.

VIGNETTING: The shading off of the space around the figure or object in print or enlargement.

WEAK: Thin, lifeless, lacking contrast, as applied to a negative.

Further Information On Any Subject In Photography.

As mentioned at the beginning of this book further information on *any* subject in photography may be obtained through correspondence with the Service Department of the Eastman Kodak Company, Rochester, N. Y.

Where helpful, constructive criticism of pictures is desired send along negatives and prints with details of how the pictures were made.

There will be no charge—no obligation.

Printed in the United States of America.